easy ENTERTAINING for *BEGINNERS*

easy ENTERTAINING *for* BEGINNERS

You can throw a fabulous party, from a holiday fiesta to a romantic evening for two

Patricia Mendez

MAPLE HEIGHTS PRESS
Torrance, CA

Published by: Maple Heights Press
P.O. Box 3936
Torrance, CA 90510
www.MapleHeightsPress.net

Publisher's Cataloging-in-Publication (Provided by Quality Books, Inc.)

Mendez, Patricia, 1958-
    Easy entertaining for beginners : you can throw a
fabulous party, from a holiday fiesta to a romantic
evening for two / Patricia Mendez.
        p. cm.
    Includes index.
    LCCN 2007940502
    ISBN-13: 978-0-9799564-0-9
    ISBN-10: 0-9799564-0-4

    1. Entertaining. 2. Cookery. 3. Menus.   I. Title.
    TX731.M46 2008   642'.4
            QBI08-600083

COVER PHOTOGRAPH: Archangel Entertainment
COVER AND INTERIOR DESIGN: Albertine Book Design
INTERIOR PHOTOGRAPHS: Martin Mendez, Rene Gonzales, and John Peirce

Dedication

To my husband, Augie, of 29 years
This book never would have been written and published
without your love, support, and practical help.
To my sons, Martin, Mario, and Alex,
for your enthusiasm, encouragement, and
willing participation in all that recipe testing!

CONTENTS

ABOUT THIS BOOK

*T*HE AMERICAN HERITAGE DICTIONARY defines the word *hospitality* as "A cordial and generous reception and treatment of guests." In our busy world, hospitality seems like an old-fashioned idea, but I believe it is a warm and effective way to connect with the ones we care about. Most people enjoy getting together with loved ones in a relaxed home environment with delicious food and drink! Plus, it is a great way to meet new people and to get to know acquaintances better.

Many people have the desire to entertain in their homes but are a bit intimidated by the task. How do I get started? What do I serve? How do I know how much to make? What if I mess it up? If these questions and others start to make you nervous, you can talk yourself out of trying in no time. I want to encourage you. Entertaining and offering hospitality to those you care about is extremely satisfying and fun. Where you lack the experience, I can help. I have designed this book with you in mind.

This book contains delicious, easy recipes that I have developed and used many times when entertaining. Each chapter includes step-by-step checklists and decorating ideas. There are 13 menus for special occasions, and every chapter has the sections "Optional Shortcuts," "Party Etiquette," "Mistakes to Avoid," and "Tips to Ensure Success." In addition, there are ideas for music and drinks, both alcoholic and nonalcoholic, that you and your guests will enjoy. This is your road map to party planning and entertaining. By all means, dive in and express your creativity in offering hospitality to your family and friends. You can do it!

GETTING STARTED

*A*S WITH ANYTHING WORTH DOING, one of the keys to success is to be prepared. In each chapter I have written a step-by-step checklist for the menu. These lists will help you pace yourself. When I was in my twenties, I would clean the house, do the shopping, prepare the food, and have the guests over in the same evening. Did I mention I was pretty exhausted by the time my guests arrived? I have learned to pace myself. I usually allow about two or three days of organized preparation for most entertaining. That may sound like a lot to you in our instant-microwave world, but it is well worth the effort. You will feel more confident and you won't be exhausted. For instance, two days before a party, I will clean the house, reread the recipes, and make a shopping list. One day before, I will do the shopping and some of the food preparation. The morning of the party, I do most of the remaining food preparation and decorating. So I spend some time each day for two to three days before a party in preparation.

The other advantage to pacing yourself in this way is that you have time to fix most of the mistakes you may make. If you are like me, you will probably make mistakes. It is not the end of the world. And the good part of making mistakes is that we usually learn from them and get to hone our skills and improve. By learning to pace yourself, you will definitely enjoy your entertaining more, and so will your guests. Now let's get into some specifics.

INVITING GUESTS

SO YOU HAVE DECIDED you want to throw a party or plan a special dinner. Think about the number of guests and who you would like to invite. Keep in mind the size of your space so everyone can be comfortable. Decide which menu you would like to use.

Not all occasions need formal invitations. Sometimes a phone call or even an e-vite (invitation via e-mail) is sufficient. Paper invitations sent via regular mail are a nice touch for a special occasion. When you have finalized your guest list, make your calls or send your invitations two to three weeks in advance. If you want a fairly accurate count of guests, make sure you ask for an RSVP. An RSVP is the favor of a reply (I can attend!) no later than five days before your gathering. This really helps with planning, so you don't underbuy or overbuy.

CHOOSING A SETTING

NEXT, DECIDE THE LOCATION OF YOUR GATHERING. You could hold the party in your backyard, dining room, or family room by the fireplace. My kitchen has an open floor plan and is located in the center of my house, and I hold many of my parties there. Decide on your location with the comfort of your guests in mind. Make it easy to access, and have enough chairs for everyone. Even at a cocktail party, where people tend to congregate around the food, most guests like to sit down at some point in the evening.

Most of the chapters in this book include simple decorating tips. You can really get creative with this and use your own touches. Don't underestimate how much a pretty table setting or some festive decorating can add to the overall mood of your party. Doing a few simple things well will show your guests that they are important to you.

Music is another way to add ambiance to the setting. Each chapter includes music suggestions that complement the theme. There are different genres, such as jazz, classical, contemporary, rock, and bluegrass. Some chapters suggest specific CDs or artists. You usually cannot go wrong if you purchase a "greatest hits" CD by one of the suggested artists. Feel free to choose music from any chapter that you and your guests will enjoy, regardless of the menu you are preparing.

SETTING A BUDGET

ONE ASPECT TO TAKE INTO CONSIDERATION when entertaining is the financial cost. This can range from a relatively low amount for small dinner parties to several hundred dollars for larger parties. If you aren't careful, expenses can start to add up when you entertain. Concentrate on the food and the table if you are on a tight budget. Use the dishes you already have for your table setting and splurge on a flower arrangement for the table to add a special touch. Lots of people have special-occasion glassware and serving items that they rarely use. Pull them out of the cupboard and enjoy them when you entertain.

Think about any extra touches you might like ahead of time to see if they work within your budget. For instance, live music or entertainment might be a fantastic addition to a party, but be aware that it can add substantially to the cost. Purchased decorations and themed paper goods can also add up. One of the themes that you will see repeated throughout this book is, "Do a few things and do them well." If you concentrate your efforts and budget with this in mind, you will pull off your entertaining with style and efficiency.

PREPARING FOR THE EVENT

START BY TAKING THE TIME TO READ THE ENTIRE CHAPTER you have chosen. Pay special attention to reading through the recipes. Make your shopping list from the ingredients listed in the dishes you will prepare. Many of the menus make use of some purchased food. With the delicious prepared foods that are available, it is a no-brainer to take advantage of these and concentrate your efforts on other menu items. For instance, in Chapter 1, "My First Cocktail Party," I suggest purchasing a tray of mini-desserts. You can pick these up from your local bakery or many warehouse stores, and nicer grocery stores have mini-pastries in the frozen food section. Feel free to substitute purchased items you know your guests will enjoy. When you are buying ingredients for recipes you will prepare, choose the freshest available. It really does make a difference in the taste.

This might seem obvious, but before you do any food preparation, make sure you wash your hands, and if you have long hair, tie it back. Set out the ingredients for the recipe you are preparing, along with measuring cups, measuring spoons, and bowls. As you prepare one recipe, quickly do the dishes before moving on to the next one. This will keep your kitchen from becoming a disaster area by the time you are finished, and you will have less cleanup at the end.

Don't be intimidated if you lack cooking experience. Recipes are simply a set of instructions. If you can follow instructions, you can accomplish a recipe. It is so rewarding to take fresh ingredients and follow a recipe to create a dish that is not only good for your health but also looks, smells, and tastes delicious. All good cooks and chefs begin the same way. They have no experience and knowledge, but by trying (and sometimes failing), they learn and develop their talent and passion for cooking and serving great cuisine. If you are hesitant to tackle an entire menu, start out by preparing one recipe at a time until you gain a bit of confidence. The steps in the recipes are designed to be as uncomplicated and easy as possible without sacrificing any flavor. You will be proud to serve your mouthwatering preparations to your guests, and you just may develop a love for cooking and entertaining along the way!

SETTING THE TONE

WHAT IS YOUR MOTIVATION FOR THROWING A PARTY or hosting a dinner in your home? My motivation is to have a way to express my love and care in a way that will be a blessing to the guests who attend. It is a gift to them to provide a few hours in a pleasant environment, with good food and gracious hospitality. The cares and concerns of everyday life will most assuredly need to be dealt with eventually, but for a few hours love, friendship, and laughter are good medicine. You want your guests to feel that of all the ways you could be spending your time, having them in your home and being with them on that occasion is exactly where you prefer to be. Does entertaining take some effort and labor? Yes, it does, but it is a labor of love. If you find a book that claims that entertaining can be accomplished effortlessly, don't believe it. I've never hosted such a gathering. If you do it right, it may *look* effortless, but that doesn't mean it didn't take some work.

So you have decided to entertain in your home. You've chosen your menu, invited your guests, and done all the preparation. It is the day of the party and your guests are scheduled to arrive. Two hours before the event is to start, take time for yourself to get dressed and ready. You have done your last-minute food prep and setup, and you have turned on the music. Take a deep breath and think for just a moment of your motivation. In short order, your guests will arrive to enjoy your warm and cordial hospitality.

AVOIDING PITFALLS

HAVE YOU EVER BEEN TO A PARTY where the host is stressed and uptight? Or is so behind schedule that she is frantically running around trying to finish the preparation as the guests are arriving? It is an uncomfortable feeling for the guests and sets the wrong tone for the party. Does this mean everything has to be perfect and there are never any stressful moments in entertaining? No, of course not. *Remember, do a few things and do them well.* If something goes wrong (the icemaker breaks, the smoke alarm goes off, one of the dishes you will serve has taken a turn for the worse), don't panic. Simply solve the problem and move on. The ability to be flexible and not let it ruin your evening is a plus. Put a smile on your face and enjoy your guests and your party. Make sure you take time to talk to each guest. Welcome each one to your home and you will immediately put them at ease. And by all means be yourself and add your own flavor and style to your entertaining. Your guests will enjoy this most of all.

THE MENUS AT A GLANCE

MY FIRST COCKTAIL PARTY
Shrimp Ceviche with Tostaditos
Seared Ahi with Lime-Cilantro Mayonnaise on Crostini
Crab-Stuffed Mushrooms
Cheese Tray
Crudités with Artichoke Dip
Assorted mini-desserts (purchased)
Cadillac Margaritas

ROMANTIC DINNER FOR TWO
Coconut Salmon with Pineapple Salsa
Aromatic Herbed Rice
Broccoli with Lemon and Parmesan
Cointreau Chocolate Truffles and Strawberries
Hurricanes

DINNER FOR THE IN-LAWS
Baby Greens with Orange-Ginger Vinaigrette
Beef Tenderloin Medallions with Savory Sauce
Baked Potatoes with Blue Cheese Dressing
Haricots Verts with Garlic and Almonds
Kahlúa Fudge Brownie Pie
Cosmopolitans

GIRLFRIENDS' TEA

Chicken Salad with Grapes and Walnuts on Mini-Croissants
English Cucumber and Cream Cheese Sandwiches
Scones
Lemon curd and strawberry jam (purchased)
Clotted Cream
Brownie Drop Cookies
Tea

MOTHER'S DAY BRUNCH

Smoked Salmon Canapés with Lemon-Dill Crème
Spinach Salad with Raspberry Vinaigrette
Sweet Crabmeat Quiche
Warm Cinnamon Rolls with Vanilla Icing
Guava Mimosas

FAMILY FIESTA

Fresh Salsa and Zesty Guacamole with purchased tortilla chips
Carne Asada
Spanish Rice
Pinto Beans with Bacon
Fresh Tomato Salad with Basil and Panela Cheese
Flour tortillas (purchased)
Paletas (frozen juice bars; purchased)
Micheladas

FOURTH OF JULY BASH

Gourmet Hamburger Bar
Tangy Dill Potato Salad
Fruit Salad with Brown Sugar–Lime Dressing
Gran's Blackberry Cobbler with Vanilla Ice Cream
French Lemonade
Strawberry Daiquiris

LITTLE GIRLS' FRIENDSHIP TEA WITH JEWELRY-MAKING CRAFT

Cucumber and Cream Cheese Sandwiches
Peanut Butter and Honey Crème Sandwiches
Chocolate-Drizzled Strawberries
Lemon Cupcakes with Cream Cheese Filling
Passion Fruit Tea

LITTLE BOYS' TRICYCLE OLYMPICS PARTY

Pizza Bar
Grapes and watermelon slices
Chocolate Cupcakes
Sparkling Punch

DINNER PARTY WITH CLOSE FRIENDS

Southwest Caesar Salad
Cornbread with Honey Butter
Chicken Tortilla Soup
Egg Custard with Strawberry Nectar
Lemon Drop Martinis

GUYS' NIGHT OUT

Hot Wings with Blue Cheese Dressing
Chili Boats with All the Fixin's
The Mega Sandwich
Smoked almonds (purchased)
Easy Cheesecake Brownies
Beer: Hefeweizen and Black & Tans

MY FIRST THANKSGIVING

Chilled Shrimp with Cocktail Sauce
Mixed nuts in the shell
Assorted cheeses and crackers
Roast Turkey with Pan Gravy

Herbed Stuffing or Apple-Pecan Stuffing
Mashed Potatoes
Butter and Brown Sugar Glazed Carrots
Crescent rolls (purchased) with butter
Pumpkin Pie with Whipped Cream

CHRISTMAS SEASON SOCIAL

Baked Brie in Crescent Dough
Buttermilk Biscuits with Ham and/or Turkey
Cheddar Hash Brown Gratin
Pear, Blue Cheese, and Candied Almond Salad with Champagne Vinaigrette
Eggnog Cake with Orange Rum Sauce
Pomegranate Sparkling Punch
Eggnog (purchased)

CHAPTER 1

MY FIRST COCKTAIL PARTY

HEN PLANNING YOUR FIRST COCKTAIL PARTY, think *simplicity*. I learned a valuable lesson with my first cocktail party. I made too many different hors d'oeuvres (small bites or munchies). I was tired by the time my party started, and I overwhelmed my guests with too much. Live and learn. Now, when I host a cocktail party, I follow the rule of simplicity. Do a few things and do them well. The tone for the party is more relaxed, and so am I.

Twelve to sixteen guests are a good, manageable number for a first cocktail party. Start with one or two different cocktails, rather than having an open bar. This really simplifies serving drinks. Choose a cocktail recipe that you can make a couple of hours before the party and serve in pitchers. That way you are not spending all your time tending bar and can visit with your guests. Offer beer and wine along with two or three nonalcoholic beverages, and have bottled water available as well. Plan to serve six or seven choices of hors d'oeuvres, at about three or four pieces each per person.

A cocktail party doesn't always need a special occasion, but it certainly is appropriate for one. A birthday, an anniversary, or even a promotion are all good reasons to throw a cocktail party. A beautiful table for the food will suffice for the extent of the decorations. I use one or two tablecloths and will sometimes put a large, sturdy box (such as one from a case of beer) under the tablecloth so the food can be placed at different heights. It is more appealing to look at than having one flat table with food on flat platters. You can always add some fresh flowers, herbs, fruit, or candles in hurricane lamps. (Be careful where you place candles, so no one can get burned when reaching for food on the table.) If you have any pretty serving platters, glasses, or even cake stands, use them.

On the menu are small bites of shrimp ceviche (pronounced say-vee-chay) served in glasses with tostaditos. A ceviche generally consists of raw fish marinated in lime or lemon juice. The citric acid "cooks" the fish, which is served in a luxurious concoction of sweet and piquant flavors. We are using cooked shrimp for this recipe, and the flavors of tomato, lime, and avocado, along with the crunchy cucumbers and jicama, are quite delicious. The ahi tuna is marinated for extra flavor, seared on the grill or under a broiler, and served on crostini (toasted slices of French baguette) with a small dollop of Lime-Cilantro Mayonnaise. The Crab-Stuffed Mushrooms are prepared in advance and are served warm. The rest of the menu consists of crudités (fresh, cut-up veggies) served with an artichoke dip, a cheese tray with assorted cheeses and crackers, and a selection of mini-desserts.

Follow the checklist and before you know it, your guests will be arriving. Seven o'clock in the evening is a great start time. As the host, be sure to introduce guests who may not know one another. It can be awkward to be the new person at a gathering when everyone else knows each other well. You can encourage conversation when making introductions by trying to offer something your guests have in common. For instance, you could say, "Mary, I would like you to meet John." "John, Mary was born and raised in your birthplace, New York City." Or offer a conversation starter with something interesting from your guest's life, such as "Mary works as a nurse at Memorial Hospital" or "Mary has run the L. A. Marathon two times." You get the picture. These attempts can encourage the start of a conversation for guests who are unfamiliar with each other.

Offer drinks and let your guests help themselves to the cold hors d'oeuvres on the table. In 20 to 30 minutes, heat one or two baking sheets of the crostini and assemble some of the hot ahi hors d'oeuvres. Pass the tray to your guests and in another 15 minutes make a few more trays. Repeat with the Crab-Stuffed Mushrooms. This way, your warm hors d'oeuvres can be offered intermittently throughout the evening. Enjoy yourself and have fun with your guests!

This menu is also appropriate for: A New Year's Eve party. Don't forget the hats, horns, noisemakers, and Champagne to ring in the New Year!

MENU

Serves 12 to 16
Shrimp Ceviche with Tostaditos
Seared Ahi with Lime-Cilantro Mayonnaise on Crostini
Crab-Stuffed Mushrooms
Cheese Tray
Crudités with Artichoke Dip
Assorted mini-desserts (purchased)

Drinks
Cadillac Margaritas
Beer
Wine: chardonnay and/or shiraz
Bottled juices or teas
Sparkling cranberry juice with lime twists
Bottled water

Music Suggestions
Justin Timberlake
As I Am by Alicia Keyes
Frank Sinatra
Michael Bublé

Shrimp Ceviche with Tostaditos

Makes 12 to 16 appetizer servings

2 pounds cooked medium shrimp (50 to 70 per pound),
*   shelled, deveined, and tails removed*
1 cup fresh lime juice (8 to 10 limes), divided
1 medium white onion, chopped
⅔ cup chopped fresh cilantro
1 cup ketchup
¼ cup bottled hot sauce, such as Cholula or Tapatio
*   (use less if you prefer a milder flavor)*
¼ cup olive oil
2 cups chopped cucumber
1 large or 2 small ripe avocados, peeled, pitted, and chopped
1 cup peeled (use a vegetable peeler), chopped jicama
*   (optional; produce section)*
About 1 teaspoon salt, or to taste
Tortilla chips (preferably a small round shape)
Lime slices or cilantro sprigs, for garnish

In a small bowl, toss the shrimp in ¾ cup of the lime juice and refrigerate for 30 minutes. In a separate bowl, mix the remaining ¼ cup lime juice, onion, cilantro, ketchup, hot sauce, olive oil, cucumber, avocado, jicama, and salt.

To serve, stir the marinated shrimp with the lime juice into the other ingredients. Spoon about 2 tablespoons of the ceviche into each small martini glass or disposable wine glass, with one or two tortilla chips (tostaditos) in each glass and a slice of lime or sprig of cilantro for garnish. These individual servings can be put on the table alongside bowls containing the remaining ceviche and tostaditos so guests can replenish their glasses. Place serving bowl of ceviche inside larger bowl filled with ice to keep chilled.

Tip: Purchase frozen cooked shrimp at a warehouse store and run under cold water in a colander to defrost for about 10 minutes; then remove the tails, if needed. It should already be deveined if you purchase it this way. Ceviche will not be good the day after the party because the lime juice will make the shrimp chewy if marinated for too long. Don't worry, there won't be any left!

Seared Ahi with Cilantro-Lime Mayonnaise on Crostini
Makes about 45 pieces

Lime-Cilantro Mayonnaise
1 cup mayonnaise
¼ cup finely chopped cilantro
1 tablespoon fresh lime juice
Salt and freshly ground black pepper to taste

Crostini
2 baguettes (long loaves of French bread)
Extra virgin olive oil

Seared Ahi
1 small onion, finely chopped
3 tablespoons fresh lime juice
⅓ cup olive oil
2 tablespoons prepared Asian chile paste (international aisle)
1 ½ pounds sashimi-quality ahi tuna
3 jalapeño chiles, sliced, for garnish (see Note)

To make the mayonnaise, mix the mayonnaise, cilantro, and lime juice together in a small bowl. Add salt and pepper to taste. Refrigerate.

To make the crostini, preheat the oven to 350 degrees F. Slice the baguettes into ¼-inch slices, place on a baking sheet, and drizzle with olive oil. Bake for 5 to 7 minutes.

To make the ahi, light a fire in a charcoal grill, or preheat a gas grill to medium-high. Mix the onion, lime juice, oil, and chile paste together in a shallow dish and add the ahi. Marinate for 30 minutes, turning once. Grill for 2 minutes. Turn and grill for 2 minutes more. You can also sear the ahi under a hot broiler for the same amount of time. The ahi will be seared on the outside and very rare on the inside. It will still have a dark pink or red color. It is very important that the grill or broiler be preheated to medium-high for proper searing. Let the ahi cool slightly, then slice thinly.

To assemble, reheat the crostini in the oven at 375 degrees F for 5 to 7 minutes. Top each with a small dollop of Lime-Cilantro Mayonnaise, a piece of ahi, and a slice of jalapeño. Serve immediately.

Tip: Sashimi-quality ahi is the freshest available and is usually used in sushi. If your guests prefer their ahi fully cooked, simply grill for 4 or 5 minutes, turn, and grill for 4 or 5 minutes more for every inch of thickness. Swordfish, albacore tuna, or shark may be substituted if ahi is unavailable.

Note: If you prefer a milder garnish, substitute sliced red bell pepper for the jalapeño.

Crab-Stuffed Mushrooms
Makes about 45 mushrooms

1 can (6 ounces) lump crabmeat, rinsed and drained well
⅓ cup unsalted butter, melted
⅓ cup breadcrumbs
¾ cup freshly grated Parmesan cheese
3 cloves garlic, finely chopped
¼ cup finely chopped onion
½ teaspoon Old Bay seasoning (spice aisle)
Salt and freshly ground black pepper to taste
3 packages (12 ounces each) fresh mushrooms
Nonstick cooking spray

In a medium bowl, mix together the crabmeat, melted butter, breadcrumbs, Parmesan, garlic, onion, Old Bay, and salt and pepper to taste. To wash the mushrooms, gently rinse them in water and dry completely. Rub off any soil particles and wiggle the stem until it breaks off, discarding the stems. Stuff the mushroom caps with the crab mixture. Refrigerate in an airtight container until ready to bake.

To bake the mushrooms, preheat the oven to 350 degrees F. Spray a baking sheet with cooking spray and place the stuffed mushrooms on the sheet. Bake for 20 minutes, until heated through.

Cheese Tray
Makes 12 to 16 appetizer servings

5 or 6 different types of cheeses, some cut up for crackers, others whole with a cheese slicer (Havarti, mild or sharp Cheddar, Gouda, Fontina, Muenster, goat cheese with herbs, blue cheese such as Gorgonzola or Stilton, Brie, Parmesan, or Asiago)
Assorted crackers
1 pound seedless grapes

Arrange the cheeses and crackers on a platter, cutting board, or cake stand with washed seedless red and green grapes in small clusters.

Tip: Most groceries stores carry a nice selection of artisan cheeses. Be creative. If you see something that looks especially good to you, try it. Arrange your cheeses on a beautiful platter, some cut up, some by the wedge with a pretty cheese knife and crackers. Try to have an assortment of soft, medium, and hard cheeses for variety: soft Brie and goat cheese; medium Havarti, Cheddar, Gouda, Fontina, and blue cheese; hard Parmesan and Asiago.

Crudités with Artichoke Dip
Makes 12 to 16 appetizer servings

Artichoke Dip
1 package (8 ounces) reduced-fat cream cheese
¼ cup light sour cream
½ cup thawed frozen artichoke hearts
½ teaspoon Worcestershire sauce
⅓ cup freshly grated Parmesan cheese
½ teaspoon grated lemon zest
1 tablespoon lemon juice
1 clove garlic, chopped
1 teaspoon salt
Freshly ground black pepper to taste

Crudités

7 or 8 stalks celery
7 or 8 carrots
4 or 5 zucchini squash
2 bunches radishes
1 English cucumber

To make the dip, add the cream cheese, sour cream, artichoke hearts, Worcestershire sauce, Parmesan cheese, lemon zest and juice, garlic, salt, and pepper to taste to a blender or food processor and blend until almost smooth.

To make the crudités, wash and trim the vegetables so the celery, carrots, cucumber, and zucchini are about 6 inches long. Cut the carrots, zucchini, and cucumber in half lengthwise, then cut them again twice more, into 8 long sticks. Store them in a zipper-lock bag and refrigerate until ready to use.

To serve, put the crudités in pretty glasses of different shapes and sizes for visual interest on the table, rather than laying them out on a platter. Serve with the dip.

Cadillac Margaritas
Makes 14-16 margaritas in two pitchers

1 bottle (1 liter) Jose Cuervo Especial (Gold) or 1800 Reposado tequila
8 cups (2 liters) Jose Cuervo Margarita Mix
10 limes
Kosher salt for rimming glasses
1 bottle (750 ml) Grand Marnier

Mix 2 cups of the tequila and 4 cups of the margarita mix in each pitcher. Squeeze the juice of 4 of the limes into each pitcher. Refrigerate. When ready to serve, cut the remaining 2 limes into slices and cut the slices in half. Reserve for garnish. Have a saucer of kosher salt ready. Rub the cut edge of a lime slice around the rim of a margarita glass. Dip the glass upside down into the salt to rim the glass. Fill with ice and the prepared tequila mixture. Place the lime slice on the rim of the glass. Leave a shot glass by the pitcher of margaritas and let your guests add a shot of Grand Marnier to the top of their glass, if desired.

Tip: The limes are easier to squeeze if they are at room temperature.

9

STEP-BY-STEP CHECKLIST

2 TO 3 WEEKS BEFORE   Invite guests.

2 DAYS BEFORE   Clean the house, reread the recipes, and make a shopping list.

1 DAY BEFORE   Shop.

Make the Lime-Cilantro Mayonnaise for the ahi hors d'oeuvre; refrigerate.

Make the Artichoke Dip; refrigerate.

Chill the drinks.

MORNING OF THE PARTY   Set up the table, glasses, and bar area.

Cut up the ingredients for Shrimp Ceviche (do not mix them together yet).

Prepare the cheese tray, cover, and refrigerate.

Prepare the ahi marinade (do not add the fish yet); refrigerate. Slice the jalapeños for garnish.

Cut up the crudités; refrigerate.

Make 2 pitchers of Cadillac Margaritas; refrigerate. Prepare the Crab-Stuffed Mushrooms (do not bake yet); refrigerate.

1 HOUR BEFORE   Set out the mini-desserts, cheese and crackers, and crudités and dip.

Put the ahi in the marinade; refrigerate.

Prepare and bake the baguette slices for crostini.

Marinate the shrimp in the lime juice; mix all of the ingredients you have previously cut for ceviche in a separate bowl.

30 MINUTES BEFORE Grill the ahi, and preheat the oven to 350 degrees F.

Add the shrimp to the ceviche. Spoon about 2 tablespoons of ceviche into each individual glass, add the garnish, and set out on the table, along with a bowl filled with extra ceviche and extra tostaditios on the side.

Turn on the music, and light candles, if using.

DURING THE PARTY Offer hot trays of ahi and stuffed mushrooms intermittently throughout the evening, every 20 minutes or so.

Reheat the crostini on a baking sheet in a 350 degree F oven for 4 to 5 minutes.

Assemble the ahi hors d'oeuvres, place on a pretty tray, and serve.

Put a baking sheet of stuffed mushrooms in the oven for 20 minutes and then assemble on a tray to serve.

Repeat throughout the evening.

11

OPTIONAL SHORTCUTS

1. If you are really pressed for time, you can purchase the some of the crudités precleaned and cut up. Many grocery stores have celery and carrot sticks in packages. To present them at their best, cut the ends off the morning of your party.

2. To save time, you can serve a favorite purchased dip with the crudités instead of making the Artichoke Dip.

PARTY ETIQUETTE

When you are hosting a party, prepare for the number of guests who have responded to the RSVP *plus* a few extra guests just in case. It's better to have extra food and drink and not need it than to need it and not have it.

MISTAKES TO AVOID

Do not prepare a new recipe that you have never made before on the day of your party. It is always a good idea to make a recipe once before your party to familiarize yourself with it. You can easily cut the recipe in half and try it a couple of weeks ahead. That way, you will be more confident on the day of your event.

TIPS TO ENSURE SUCCESS

Save a lot of money by purchasing your alcoholic beverages at a warehouse store. You can get a larger size for the same amount you would pay for a small size at the grocery store.

CHAPTER 2

ROMANTIC DINNER FOR TWO

*I*F YOU ARE TRYING TO DECIDE WHICH MENU in this book would be the easiest to start with, I recommend this chapter. First of all, you will only be cooking for two, and the menu is an easy one to prepare. Tempt your guest with a frosty Hurricane. This tropically inspired drink is made with dark rum, orange juice, pineapple juice, and a splash of grenadine (pomegranate syrup). The salmon recipe is a light yet delicious seafood entrée baked with a crunchy coconut coating that pairs perfectly with the pineapple salsa. The aromatic herbed rice is simple yet flavorful. Fresh broccoli is available in every season and is a breeze to prepare. The Cointreau Chocolate Truffles are simply decadent, and their rich sweetness is offset by serving them alongside fresh strawberries.

I have tried to avoid the cliché of foods that are supposed to jumpstart your libido that you find in most menus for romantic meals and instead focus on tasty food made with the freshest ingredients. After all, the real romance is the love you are demonstrating by creating a special evening just for the two of you. It is in quiet moments like these that you can unwind, connect, and recharge.

For your setting, choose music that you both enjoy. You can also try some of the music suggestions listed after the menu. Low lighting and unscented candles set a relaxing mood. Feel free to eat at the dining table or at a coffee table set in front of the fireplace—wherever you are most comfortable. If you have children, either hire a trustworthy babysitter (preferably at a different location) or order pizza for the kids' dinner and put them to bed for the evening before enjoying your dinner for two.

MENU

Serves 2

Coconut Salmon with Pineapple Salsa

Aromatic Herbed Rice

Broccoli with Lemon and Parmesan

Cointreau Chocolate Truffles and Strawberries

Drinks

Hurricanes or sparkling wine

Music Suggestions

Siempre by Il Divo

Get Lifted by John Legend

Coconut Salmon
Makes 2 servings

Nonstick cooking spray
⅓ cup cornstarch
¾ teaspoon salt
¼ to ½ teaspoon ground cayenne pepper
2 large egg whites
1 ½ cups sweetened flaked coconut (baking aisle)
1 pound salmon fillet, skinless, wild caught or, if not available, farm raised

Preheat the oven to 375 degrees F. Spray a baking sheet with cooking spray. Combine the cornstarch, salt, and cayenne in a shallow dish. In a medium bowl with an electric mixer, beat the egg whites on medium-high speed until white and frothy, about 2 minutes. Put the coconut in a separate shallow dish.
Cut the salmon into 2 pieces. Wash and dry with a paper towel. Coat each piece of salmon with the cornstarch mixture, then with the egg whites, and then with the coconut. Place on the baking sheet.

Cover with aluminum foil and bake for 15 minutes. Uncover and bake for 10 to 12 minutes more, depending on the thickness of the fish, until the flesh is no longer red but pink and flaky and the coconut is browned. Do not overcook.

Tip: To separate the egg white from the yolk, crack an egg in half over a bowl and let the white part of the egg fall into the bowl. Keep the yolk in the shell and do not let any get into the white part. Carefully pour the yolk into the other half of the shell and let the remaining white drip into the bowl. Discard the yolk or save for another use. Repeat with the second egg.

Pineapple Salsa
Makes about 1 ½ cups

1 cup finely chopped fresh pineapple
¼ cup chopped cilantro
¼ cup finely chopped red onion
1 jalapeño chile, finely chopped
½ red bell pepper, seeds removed, finely chopped
Juice of 1 lime
Dash of bottled hot sauce, such as Tapatio or Cholula
Salt and freshly ground black pepper to taste

In a medium bowl, combine the pineapple, cilantro, onion, jalapeño, bell pepper, lime juice, hot sauce, and salt and pepper to taste. Cover and refrigerate until ready to use. Serve alongside or on top of the salmon.

Tip: To clean a fresh pineapple, cut off the green top, along with about 1 inch of the top of the pineapple. Cut 1 inch from the bottom of the pineapple. Cut the pineapple in half lengthwise and then in half lengthwise again to have 4 quarters. Hold a quarter on its end and cut about an inch off the middle; this is the core. Then, with a jiggling motion, cut off the rind of the pineapple, discarding it. Finely chop the pineapple flesh until you have 1 cup. You can cut some wedges from the remaining pineapple to garnish the Hurricanes and save the rest for another use. Try it sprinkled with salt for a great fresh snack.

Aromatic Herbed Rice

Makes 2 servings

2 tablespoons canola oil
2 cloves garlic, finely chopped
¾ cup uncooked jasmine rice
1 ½ cups hot water
1 sprig fresh thyme (produce section)
1 sprig fresh oregano (produce section)
1 bay leaf
2 teaspoons finely chopped cilantro or flat-leaf (Italian) parsley
Salt and freshly ground black pepper to taste

Heat the oil in a medium saucepan over medium heat, add the garlic, and cook for 1 to 2 minutes, until fragrant. Add the rice and cook, stirring constantly, for about 1 minute. Add the hot water, thyme, oregano, and bay leaf. Cover and simmer over low heat for about 20 minutes, or until all of the water is absorbed. Turn off the heat and let the rice sit for 3 to 4 minutes. Remove the bay leaf and the thyme and oregano sprigs. Stir in the cilantro and salt and pepper to taste right before serving.

17

Broccoli with Lemon and Parmesan

Makes 2 servings

8 ounces fresh broccoli florets
1 tablespoon fresh lemon juice
1 tablespoon unsalted butter, softened to room temperature
2 tablespoons freshly grated Parmesan cheese
Salt and freshly ground black pepper to taste

Wash and trim the broccoli until the florets are about 2 inches in length. Pour 1 inch of water into a medium saucepan, add the broccoli, cover, and cook over medium heat for 5 to 6 minutes, or until the broccoli is just tender when speared with a fork. Drain well in a colander. In a serving bowl, combine the broccoli, lemon juice, butter, and Parmesan cheese. Toss carefully until the butter melts, and add salt and pepper to taste. Serve immediately.

Cointreau Chocolate Truffles and Strawberries
Makes about 18 truffles

6 ounces semisweet chocolate, chopped (baking aisle)
½ cup heavy cream
2 tablespoons Cointreau (a French orange liqueur)
Chocolate sprinkles and/or unsweetened cocoa powder for coating the truffles
1 pint fresh strawberries, washed

Chop the chocolate and place in a medium oven-safe bowl. Heat the heavy cream in a small saucepan until just boiling and pour over the chocolate. Stir to melt the chocolate. If necessary, you can put the bowl in the microwave for 30 seconds at a time to finish melting all the chocolate. Add the Cointreau, stir, and let cool at room temperature for about 10 minutes. Cover and refrigerate for 45 to 60 minutes, or until the mixture is chilled and you are able to scoop it with a teaspoon. It should be the consistency of fudge.

Cover a baking sheet with a piece of waxed paper. Scoop out some of the chocolate mixture with a teaspoon and, using your hands, roll it quickly into a small ball. Or if you have a small melon baller, you can use it to scoop out the chocolate. Place on the baking sheet. If the mixture is still too soft, refrigerate for 10 more minutes and then roll into balls. Roll the truffles in chocolate sprinkles or cocoa powder to coat. Store in a covered container in the refrigerator. Serve alongside the strawberries.

Tip: A melon baller looks like a very small ice cream scoop and can be found in any cooking store or most discount stores in the housewares section. You can also use it for the fruit salad in Chapter 6, "Fourth of July Bash."

Hurricane
Makes 1 drink

½ cup pineapple juice
¼ cup orange juice
3 tablespoons dark rum
Splash of grenadine (liquor aisle or liquor store)
Wedge of pineapple for garnish

Chill all of the ingredients beforehand. Pour the pineapple juice and orange juice into a tall glass. Pour the rum in slowly, on top of a teaspoon held over the glass to diffuse it so it will float on top of the juices. Add a splash of grenadine. Garnish with a wedge of pineapple. Serve with a swizzle stick so your guest can stir it all together.

STEP-BY-STEP CHECKLIST

2 DAYS BEFORE   Reread the recipes and make a shopping list.

1 DAY BEFORE   Shop.

Prepare the Cointreau Chocolate Truffles; refrigerate.

MORNING OF THE DINNER   Set the table.

Chill the drink ingredients.

Prepare the Pineapple Salsa, cover, and refrigerate.

1 HOUR BEFORE   Wash and cut the broccoli florets, grate the Parmesan cheese; set aside.

Prepare the cornstarch mixture for the salmon.

Wash, dry, and cut the salmon into 2 pieces.

45 MINUTES BEFORE   Preheat the oven to 375 degrees F.

Beat the egg whites, and prepare the salmon for baking.

30 MINUTES BEFORE   Bake the salmon.

Cook the rice.

10 MINUTES BEFORE	Make the Hurricanes.
	Cook the broccoli.
	Turn on the music, and light candles, if using.
AT DINNER	Serve the salmon with the pineapple salsa.
	Toss all ingredients for the broccoli; serve.
	Serve the herbed rice.
SOMETIME DURING THE EVENING	Serve the truffles with the strawberries.

OPTIONAL SHORTCUTS

1. You may purchase truffles instead of making them yourself.

2. You may purchase a container of fresh, cut-up pineapple in the produce section of the grocery store instead of cutting your own.

PARTY ETIQUETTE

It is always polite to use good table manners, including chewing with your mouth closed when eating and swallowing your food before speaking.

MISTAKES TO AVOID

Don't overcook the broccoli, or it will turn to mush.

TIPS TO ENSURE SUCCESS

Do not purchase Parmesan cheese in a can. For better flavor, purchase a fresh wedge and grate it. If you can find Parmigiano Reggiano (imported from Italy), use that for outstanding flavor. If not, regular Parmesan will suffice.

CHAPTER 3

DINNER FOR THE IN-LAWS

*T*HIS MENU, WHILE ABSOLUTELY DELICIOUS AND ELEGANT, is almost all done completely in advance. With the exception of pan-frying the beef medallions and a 4- to 5-minute stir-fry of the haricots verts, everything will be done when your in-laws arrive, leaving you less rushed and more relaxed. Start mom and dad off with a Cosmopolitan and some enjoyable music. Trust me—most family dinners are done at the parents' home, so this will be a welcome treat for your in-laws. It will open the way for some fun, intimate conversation and promote goodwill and love in your relationship.

If you have a beautiful tablecloth, use it for this setting. Use cloth napkins and placemats if you have them, and your best dishware. Set out the silverware and the salad plates in individual place settings. Put the dinner plates in the kitchen, since you will be plating this dinner individually. Fresh flowers in a low vase would be a lovely addition, and if you would like to use candles, be sure they are unscented. Scented candles interfere with the fragrance of the food and even one's sense of taste. Don't forget salt and pepper on the table and a glass of water for each person in addition to a wine glass, if serving wine.

This menu is also appropriate for: Dinner with business associates, an adult birthday party (purchase a birthday cake), or a dinner with close friends.

MENU

Serves 4

Baby Greens with Orange-Ginger Vinaigrette
Beef Tenderloin Medallions with Savory Sauce
Baked Potatoes with Blue Cheese Dressing
Haricots Verts with Garlic and Almonds
Kahlúa Fudge Brownie Pie

Drinks

Cosmopolitans
Wine: merlot, cabernet sauvignon, Bordeaux

Music Suggestions

Diana Krall
River: The Joni Letters by Herbie Hancock

Baby Greens
with Orange-Ginger Vinaigrette
Makes 4 servings

Salad
4 cups mixed baby greens
2 seedless oranges, preferably mandarin

Orange-Ginger Vinaigrette
¼ cup extra virgin olive oil
¼ cup peanut oil
Finely grated zest of 1 orange
3 tablespoons fresh orange juice
1 tablespoon grated peeled fresh ginger (produce section)
1 tablespoon finely chopped seeded jalapeño chile
½ teaspoon sugar
Salt and freshly ground black pepper to taste

To make the salad, make sure the salad greens are washed and dried, and put them in a salad bowl. Keep in the refrigerator until ready to toss with the vinaigrette. Peel the oranges and divide them into sections. Arrange on top of the salad.

To make the vinaigrette, whisk together the olive and peanut oils, orange zest and juice, grated ginger, jalapeño, sugar, and salt and pepper to taste.

To serve, toss about half of the vinaigrette with the greens. Serve on individual salad plates.

Tip: For orange zest, wash and dry an orange. Using the smallest holes on a grater, grate the orange part of the skin. Keep turning the orange on the grater to get all the zest. Avoid grating the white part of the skin because it is bitter. You can zest lemons and limes in this way also.

Beef Tenderloin Medallions
with Savory Sauce
Makes 4 servings

Savory Sauce
1 tablespoon olive oil
1 clove garlic, finely chopped
2 tablespoons finely chopped red onion
1 ½ tablespoons stone-ground mustard
1 cup beef broth (soup aisle)
1 tablespoon tomato paste (not sauce)
2 tablespoons real maple syrup
2 tablespoons cider vinegar
1 bay leaf
1 teaspoon salt
Freshly ground black pepper to taste

Steaks
2 to 2 ½ pounds beef tenderloin, trimmed and
    cut into eight ½-inch-thick steaks
Olive oil
Salt and freshly ground black pepper to taste
1 tablespoon chopped cilantro, for garnish

To make the sauce, heat the olive oil in a small sauté pan over medium heat. Add the garlic and onion and sauté for 1 or 2 minutes. Add the mustard, beef broth, tomato paste, maple syrup, cider vinegar, bay leaf, salt, and pepper. Simmer for 8 to 10 minutes over low heat, until the sauce thickens slightly. Turn off the heat, and cover until ready to use.

To prepare the steaks, brush them with olive oil and season with salt and pepper. Cover and let rest at room temperature. When ready to cook, preheat a large frying pan over medium heat. Add the steaks and pan-fry for 2 to 3 minutes. Turn and cook for another 1 or 2 minutes.

To serve, place 2 steaks on each plate, spoon some of the sauce over them, and sprinkle the chopped cilantro on top.

Tip: The biggest mistake you can make is to overcook the tenderloin. You really want it cooked no more than medium (pink in the center) for optimum flavor and tenderness.

Baked Potatoes
with Blue Cheese Dressing
Makes 4 servings

4 medium baking potatoes (Idaho or russet)

Blue Cheese Dressing
½ cup mayonnaise
½ cup light sour cream
⅓ cup crumbled blue cheese
1 teaspoon cider vinegar
Dash of bottled hot sauce, such as Cholula or Tapatio
1 teaspoon Worcestershire sauce
1 teaspoon finely chopped shallot
2 cloves garlic, finely chopped
2 teaspoons chopped flat-leaf (Italian) parsley
Salt and freshly ground black pepper to taste

Wash and dry the potatoes, and stab each one several times with a fork. Wrap in aluminum foil. Refrigerate until ready to bake.

To make the dressing, combine the mayonnaise and sour cream in a medium bowl. Fold in the blue cheese, vinegar, hot sauce, Worcestershire sauce, shallot, garlic, parsley, and salt and pepper to taste. Refrigerate until ready to serve.

To bake the potatoes, preheat the oven to 350 degrees F. Bake the potatoes for 60 to 75 minutes, or until a potato is soft when you squeeze it (with an oven mitt). Serve with the blue cheese dressing alongside.

Tips: The reason you stab the potato with a fork is to allow steam to escape so it will not explode in your oven. Shallots are members of the onion family and are found in the produce section of your grocery store, by the onions and garlic.

Haricots Verts with Garlic and Almonds
Makes 4 servings

1 pound fresh haricots verts or regular green beans
¾ cup water
2 tablespoons olive oil
2 or 3 cloves garlic, finely chopped
Salt and freshly ground black pepper to taste
¼ cup sliced almonds

Wash the beans. Cut off the stem on the end of each bean. Put the beans in a large sauté pan with the water. Bring to a boil, cover, and simmer on low heat for 4 to 5 minutes. Check the water level once, and add a little more if needed. Stick a fork in a bean. When done, it should be crispy tender—not too hard and not too mushy. If you use regular green beans, you will have to increase the cooking time by 2 or 3 minutes. Empty the beans into a colander and rinse with cold water to stop the cooking. Drain well, cover, and put in the refrigerator until ready to stir-fry at the last minute.

To stir-fry the beans, heat the olive oil in a large frying pan over medium heat and add the garlic. Cook, stirring constantly, for 1 or 2 minutes. Do not let the garlic get brown; it should only become fragrant and flavor the oil. Add the reserved green beans and stir to coat with the oil and garlic. Continue stirring for 3 to 4 minutes, or until heated through. Season with salt and pepper, sprinkle with the almonds, and serve.

Tip: What is a haricot vert? It is essentially a French green bean, picked while young and tender. If you can't find these, regular green beans can be substituted.

Kahlúa Fudge Brownie Pie
Makes 6 servings

½ box fudge brownie mix (about 2 cups)
⅓ cup hot water
2 teaspoons vanilla extract, divided
1 large egg
Nonstick cooking spray
1 small jar fudge ice cream topping
¾ cup low-fat milk
3 tablespoons Kahlúa (coffee-flavored liqueur)
1 package (3.9 ounces) chocolate instant pudding and pie filling mix
3 cups whipped topping, divided

Preheat the oven to 325 degrees F. In a medium bowl, combine the brownie mix, hot water, 1 teaspoon of the vanilla, and the egg. Coat a 9-inch pie pan with cooking spray, and pour the mixture into the pan. Bake for 20 to 22 minutes. Let cool completely. When cooled, spread the fudge ice cream topping on top of the brownie crust, about ¼ inch thick.

Combine the milk, 2 tablespoons of the Kahlúa, the remaining 1 teaspoon vanilla, and pudding mix in a small bowl. Whisk or beat with an electric mixer for 1 minute. Fold in 1 ½ cups of the whipped topping. Spread the pudding mixture over the brownie crust.

Combine the remaining 1 tablespoon Kahlúa and 1 ½ cups whipped topping and spread over the pudding mixture. Refrigerate until ready to serve.

Cosmopolitans
Makes 4 drinks

1 ½ cups cranberry juice
¾ cup vodka
½ cup Triple Sec or Cointreau
½ cup fresh lime juice (4 or 5 limes)
Lime wedges and fresh cranberries or cherries, for garnish

Pour the cranberry juice, vodka, Triple Sec, and lime juice into a pitcher, mix well, and refrigerate.

To serve, pour the chilled mixture into martini glasses and garnish with a decorative toothpick with a wedge of lime and a fresh cranberry or cherry.

STEP-BY-STEP CHECKLIST

2 DAYS BEFORE Clean the house, reread the recipes, and make a shopping list.

1 DAY BEFORE Shop.

Chill the drinks.

Make the Kahlúa Fudge Brownie Pie; refrigerate.

MORNING OF THE DINNER Make the Orange-Ginger Vinaigrette; refrigerate.

Clean, cut up, and parboil the haricots verts; refrigerate.

Chop 6 cloves of garlic (3 for the haricots verts, 1 for the savory sauce, and 2 for the blue cheese dressing). Cover and refrigerate until ready to use.

Prep the potatoes; refrigerate until ready to use.

Prepare the blue cheese dressing, cover, and refrigerate.

Prepare the Cosmopolitan mix in a pitcher; refrigerate.

Set the table.

1 HOUR BEFORE Make the savory sauce.

Season the steaks, and set them out at room temperature, covered.

Put the baby greens in a salad bowl, cover, and refrigerate.

Preheat the oven and bake the potatoes.

AS GUESTS ARRIVE

Turn on the music, and light candles, if using.

Serve the drinks.

Check the potatoes.

15 MINUTES AFTER ARRIVAL

Toss the salad with the vinaigrette and serve.

Put the blue cheese dressing and butter on the table.

Pan-fry the steaks and warm the sauce over very low heat.

Stir-fry the haricots verts, and sprinkle with sliced almonds.

Plate the steaks, baked potatoes, and haricots verts.

Pour the sauce over the steaks and garnish with chopped cilantro. Serve.

SOMETIME DURING THE EVENING

Serve the Kahlúa Fudge Brownie pie with coffee, if desired.

OPTIONAL SHORTCUTS

1. You can purchase a chocolate cream pie from a bakery instead of baking the Kahlúa Fudge Brownie Pie.

2. You can purchase baby salad greens already washed in a bag in the produce section.

PARTY ETIQUETTE

Turn off your cell phones or put them on vibrate mode. Turn on your answering service or voicemail and try to avoid being on the telephone when you entertain.

MISTAKES TO AVOID

Don't compare yourself to your mother-in-law. She has had lots of years of practice and started out the same as other young wives. If you struggle at all with competitiveness or insecurity, throw it out for the evening. Remember, you are giving a gift to your in-laws of a lovely meal and gracious hospitality. Who doesn't appreciate that?

TIPS TO ENSURE SUCCESS

This entrée is a good one to plate individually. First, serve the salad at the table, and then arrange the haricots verts, potato, and Beef Tenderloin Medallions with Savory Sauce on the dinner plates and garnish with the cilantro. Make it look neat and appealing to the eye and serve your guests their entrée already plated.

CHAPTER 4

GIRLFRIENDS' TEA

*T*AKING TEA EVERY AFTERNOON IS A PLEASANT CUSTOM practiced in many parts of the world. My maternal grandparents emigrated from Germany in the 1920s. They brought some of their European customs with them, including a daily teatime. I have many happy childhood memories of visits with my grandparents. A full-course dinner was served every day promptly at 11 a.m. Tea and some type of sweet baked good followed in the afternoon, with supper being a simple meal of a sandwich in the evening. I have continued to enjoy the practice of afternoon tea in my own life, but sadly, I have had to leave the daily sweet treat behind. Oh, to be young again and eat whatever I want!

Holding a tea party in your home is lots of fun. Teas can also be held in a garden or backyard with flowers. Essentially, teatime involves using pretty teacups, plates, simple food, and, of course, tea! You will prepare finger food with flavors that are not complicated but, rather, fresh and straightforward. For example, a scone is a lightly sweetened biscuit that is served with jam or lemon curd and clotted cream. Two o'clock p.m. is a good time for a tea party. The finger foods are meant to hold you over until supper, not be a huge meal in themselves. Offering your friendship and hospitality with the tinkling of teacups is a little gift of luxury you can give to your friends and yourself.

You can consider giving a small gift to your guests at your tea. Perhaps a special teacup with some delicious teabags or a small gift of flowers. My girlfriend and I hosted a tea for our friend's baby shower. We purchased inexpensive votive candle holders that were shaped like little ceramic baskets. We soaked small pieces of floral foam in water and pushed flowers into the foam to cover the top of the votive. There were about 20 guests at that tea, so we placed the "baskets" all around my house for decoration, and the ladies were delighted when we offered each of them one to take home at the end of the tea. This is totally optional, but sometimes unexpected touches can make your event more special.

Set up your table with a pretty tablecloth—pastel, floral, or white, if you have one—and napkins. Use any matched or mismatched teacups, along with a teapot, sugar cubes, and little wedges of lemon for the tea. Fresh flowers are so beautiful at a tea, and a bouquet in a pitcher or crystal vase works well. If you have any crystal or silver, a tea is a perfect time to use it. If not, use what you have and the food will be the main focal point.

This menu is also appropriate for: Mother's Day, a baby or bridal shower, or a female birthday (make Lemon Cupcakes with Cream Cheese Filling from Chapter 8, or purchase cupcakes).

MENU

Serves 10 to 12
Chicken Salad with Grapes and Walnuts on Mini-Croissants
English Cucumber and Cream Cheese Sandwiches
Scones
Lemon curd and strawberry jam (purchased)
Clotted Cream
Brownie Drop Cookies
Tea

Music Suggestions
Italia by Chris Botti
Put Your Records On by Corinne Bailey Rae

Chicken Salad with Grapes and Walnuts on Mini-Croissants
Makes 24 small sandwiches

*Meat from 1 precooked rotisserie chicken (available at most grocery stores),
     skinned, boned, and shredded, or Basic Chicken, page 164*
1 cup seedless grapes, washed and cut in half
1 cup chopped walnuts
½ cup finely chopped celery (about 2 stalks)
1 cup mayonnaise
Salt and freshly ground black pepper to taste
2 dozen mini-croissants or small rolls
Small grape clusters, for garnish

To make the chicken salad, in a medium bowl, mix together the shredded chicken, grape halves, walnuts, celery, and mayonnaise. Add salt and pepper to taste. Refrigerate, covered, until ready to assemble.

To assemble, spread the chicken salad on the mini-croissants and arrange on a platter, with clusters of washed grapes as a garnish.

Tip: Always wash fresh produce before use to remove any dirt or pesticide residue that may remain on it. Dry with a paper towel.

37

English Cucumber and Cream Cheese Sandwiches
Makes about 40 small sandwiches

1 English (seedless) cucumber
Salt
1 package (8 ounces) cream cheese, softened to room temperature
1 loaf white bread

Slice the cucumber thinly. Arrange the slices on paper towels. Salt lightly and allow to drain for about 10 minutes. Spread the cream cheese on the bread and top with cucumber slices. Either slice the crusts off the bread and cut into 4 triangles or use a small cookie cutter (like a flower shape) to cut out the sandwiches. Cover and refrigerate until ready to serve.

Scones
Makes 12 scones

4 cups all-purpose unbleached flour
2 tablespoons baking powder
¼ cup sugar
1 teaspoon salt
¾ cup cold unsalted butter (1 ½ sticks)
1 ½ cups buttermilk
1 egg
1 teaspoon water

Preheat the oven to 425 degrees F. In a large bowl, mix together the flour, baking powder, sugar, and salt. Cut the butter into small pieces and cut it into the dry ingredients. To do this, use a pastry cutter or 2 butter knives and, using a crossing motion, keep cutting the butter into smaller pieces and blending it with the flour mixture until it is the size of small peas. Pour in the buttermilk and stir until a dough forms. If the dough is too dry, add more buttermilk, 1 tablespoon at a time. For tender scones, do not overmix.

Turn half of the dough out onto a floured surface and shape it into a 6-inch circle. Cut it into 6 wedges and place on an ungreased baking sheet, 2 inches apart. Repeat with the other half of the dough, for a total of 12 scones. For the egg wash, slightly beat the egg with the water in a small bowl. Using a pastry brush, lightly paint the top of each scone for a nice golden brown sheen after baking. Discard any unused egg wash. Bake for 18 to 20 minutes, until light brown.

Tip: If you do not have buttermilk, substitute 1 ½ cups whole milk and 1 ½ tablespoons lemon juice or white vinegar. Mix together and let sit for 5 minutes before using.

Faux Clotted Cream
Makes about 1 ½ cups

½ cup heavy cream
2 tablespoons powdered sugar
½ cup sour cream

Beat the heavy cream with an electric mixer until medium-stiff peaks form. In the last few minutes of beating, add the powdered sugar. Turn the mixer off and, with a spatula, gently fold in the sour cream. Cover and refrigerate. Serve with the scones, alongside lemon curd and strawberry jam.

Brownie Drop Cookies
Makes 3 dozen cookies

2 bars (4 ounces each) Baker's German's Sweet Chocolate (baking aisle)
1 tablespoon unsalted butter
2 eggs
⅔ cup sugar
¾ teaspoon vanilla
¼ cup all-purpose unbleached flour
¼ teaspoon baking powder
⅛ teaspoon salt
¾ cup chopped walnuts
Nonstick cooking spray

Preheat the oven to 350 degrees F. Break up the chocolate into pieces and place in a microwave-safe bowl with the butter. Microwave on high power for 1 minute. Stir and, if all of the chocolate is melted, set aside to cool. If not, microwave for 15 more seconds, stir, and set aside to cool.

In a medium mixing bowl, with a hand mixer, beat the eggs until foamy (about 20 seconds). Add the sugar to the eggs, 2 tablespoons at a time, while beating the mixture. Continue adding the sugar slowly until all is added and beat for 4 to 5 minutes, until thick and creamy. Add the vanilla.

In a separate bowl, mix together the flour, baking powder, and salt. Blend the chocolate and butter mixture into the egg mixture until smooth. With a spoon, add the flour mixture and stir together. Fold in the chopped walnuts and drop the batter by teaspoonfuls onto a cold baking sheet sprayed with cooking spray. Bake for 12 to 14 minutes, until the tops are cracked and shiny. Let cool, then wrap with plastic wrap until ready to serve.

Tea

4 cups boiling water for each pot of tea
1 box teabags, such as Earl Grey, Ceylon, or any black tea
1 box herbal teabags, such as Tazo Passionfruit, chamomile, or orange spice (no caffeine)

Pour the water into a pretty ceramic teapot and add 3 teabags. Let sit (steep) for 4 to 5 minutes. Take out the teabags and serve immediately.

STEP-BY-STEP CHECKLIST

2 DAYS BEFORE — Clean the house, reread the recipes, and make a shopping list.

1 DAY BEFORE — Shop (don't forget sugar cubes and 1 lemon for tea).

Prepare the Brownie Drop Cookies; cool and cover tightly with plastic wrap.

Shred the chicken; refrigerate in an airtight container.

MORNING OF THE TEA — Set the table.

Make the chicken salad; refrigerate.

Make the scones; cool and wrap in plastic wrap.

Slice and salt the cucumbers, and drain on paper towels; cover tightly and refrigerate.

Make the clotted cream; cover and refrigerate.

Set out the cream cheese to soften to room temperature.

1 HOUR BEFORE — Assemble the chicken salad sandwiches; cover.

Assemble the cucumber and cream cheese sandwiches; cover.

Set out the lemon curd, strawberry jam, sugar cubes, and lemon wedges.

41

Put the cookies on a pretty tray, and set out (covered until serving).

Turn on the music.

Uncover all food.

Heat the water for tea and serve.

Set out the clotted cream.

OPTIONAL SHORTCUTS

1. You can purchase cookies and/or scones from a bakery instead of baking them.

PARTY ETIQUETTE

In the past, people would play simple parlor games when they socialized in each other's homes. It was considered good manners and thoughtful hospitality for the host to offer a clever or entertaining game so guests could join in the merriment. A tea is an ideal occasion for you to offer a fun parlor game. The Minister's Cat is a game from the Victorian era. The host starts out by saying, "The minister's cat is a _____ cat." Fill in the blank with an adjective that starts with the letter *A*, such as "The Minister's cat is an *adorable* cat." The next guest must quickly say the same thing and come up with a different adjective that starts with the letter *A* ("The Minister's cat is an *angry* cat"). Repeat around the room as each guest quickly says the same thing as the host but comes up with a different adjective starting with the letter *A*. When it gets back around to the host, she starts over, except using an adjective beginning with the letter *B* to describe the cat. If someone cannot think of an adjective, she is out of the game. The play continues quickly around the room and down the alphabet until the last quick-thinking person in the game is the winner.

43

TIPS TO ENSURE SUCCESS

Most people don't have several different sets of dishes to use for all these different occasions. I have one full set of my everyday dishware. I also purchased an inexpensive set of all-white dishware for eight from a discount store, and I have odds and ends from other sets of dishes. I have pink floral lunch plates from an incomplete set of my great-grandmother's china. I have bread plates and soup bowls with a turkey pattern in blue and white, and I have some bowls and salad plates with a Southwest feel to them. I mix and match these incomplete sets with my full set of white dishware when I want a different look for different occasions. For instance, for a tea I will use the floral lunch plates and mismatched teacups with some of the white dishware. For Thanksgiving I will use the turkey plates for bread and set them on top of the white dinner plates when setting the table, for a festive look. And when I have a very large gathering, I can use my everyday dishware plus the white dishware together. You can have a variety of looks without having to invest in lots of different dinnerware.

MISTAKES TO AVOID

Do not assemble the sandwiches more than 1 hour ahead, or the bread will be soggy.

CHAPTER 5

MOTHER'S DAY BRUNCH

BRUNCH IS A CROSS BETWEEN BREAKFAST AND LUNCH and is normally served anywhere from 11 a.m. to 2 p.m. Mother's Day is a lovely occasion for such a gathering. This menu is refined and set apart from the everyday. Yet it is simple enough for you to prepare and show your mother that you think she is also set apart from the ordinary.

Offer your mom and other guests a Guava Mimosa made from Champagne and guava juice served in a sugar-rimmed champagne flute or wine glass. Or serve nonalcoholic spritzers of guava juice and lemon-lime soda or club soda. Serving this beverage alongside the Smoked Salmon Canapés suggests immediately that you are celebrating a very special occasion. The canapés are served on buttered pumpernickel toasts with lemon-dill crème and a slice of smoked salmon. Serve the crunchy Spinach Salad with Raspberry Vinaigrette on a chilled salad plate, alongside a slice of the delicate Sweet Crabmeat Quiche. Top that off with the aroma of freshly baked Warm Cinnamon Rolls with Vanilla Icing and your guests will think they are dining in a fine restaurant. Of course, in a fine restaurant they would not have the privilege of dining with the chef, as they will in your extraordinary establishment!

Since Mother's Day is a special occasion, use a cloth tablecloth if you have one, or purchase one that will complement your dishware. This can give your table an elegant look. Use cloth napkins and china if you have them. Either pick a bouquet of flowers from your own flower beds or purchase some beautiful tulips or daffodils and place them in a low vase on the table. After cutting the stems on an angle, add 1 teaspoon of sugar and 2 drops of household bleach to the water. This will help your cut flowers last longer. Arrange a few small framed photographs of your mom in a grouping by the floral centerpiece. Have her baby photo, high school graduation photo, or other memorable photos displayed for a nostalgic touch.

This menu is also appropriate for: Sunday brunch or a bridal or baby shower.

MENU

Serves 6 to 8
Smoked Salmon Canapés with Lemon-Dill Crème
Spinach Salad with Raspberry Vinaigrette
Sweet Crabmeat Quiche
Warm Cinnamon Rolls with Vanilla Icing

Drinks
Guava Mimosas
Assorted juices, such as guava, mango, and pineapple-orange
Freshly brewed coffee

Music
Come Away with Me by Norah Jones

Smoked Salmon Canapés
with Lemon-Dill Crème

Makes 20 to 24 canapés

10 to 12 thin slices rye or pumpernickel bread
2 tablespoons unsalted butter, softened to room temperature
½ cup light sour cream
¼ cup light cream cheese, softened to room temperature
¼ teaspoon grated lemon zest
1 teaspoon lemon juice
1 teaspoon chopped fresh dill, or ½ teaspoon dried
8 ounces smoked salmon, thinly sliced into ½-inch strips
22 small sprigs fresh dill, for garnish

Preheat the oven to 325 degrees F. Arrange the slices of bread on a baking sheet. Spread very lightly with butter and toast in the oven for 4 to 5 minutes. Turn the slices over with a spatula and toast for another 4 minutes. Let cool. Cut out 2 small rounds per slice with a 1 ½-inch round cookie or biscuit cutter or a small drinking glass, or cut 2-inch squares with a knife.

Mix the sour cream, cream cheese, lemon zest and juice, and chopped dill in a small bowl. Arrange the toasts on a pretty platter. Spoon a small dollop of lemon-dill crème on each toast. Place a salmon slice on top and garnish with a sprig of fresh dill. Serve immediately.

47

Spinach Salad with Raspberry Vinaigrette

Makes 6 to 8 servings

Salad

3 slices bacon
8 cups fresh baby spinach leaves
1 pint fresh raspberries, carefully rinsed and drained
½ small red onion, thinly sliced and separated into rings
½ English (seedless) cucumber, peeled and thinly sliced

Raspberry Vinaigrette

2 tablespoons seedless raspberry jam
2 tablespoons white wine vinegar
1 tablespoon sugar or honey
3 tablespoons olive oil

To make the salad, fry the bacon slices in a skillet until very crisp. Drain on paper towels and let cool completely. When cool, crush with your hands into small pieces. Combine the spinach, raspberries, onion, cucumber, and bacon pieces in a large salad bowl.

To make the raspberry vinaigrette, in a small bowl, whisk together the jam, vinegar, honey, and oil. Toss with the salad and serve immediately.

Sweet Crabmeat Quiche

Makes 6 to 8 servings

2 tablespoons dry breadcrumbs
½ cup shredded Monterey Jack cheese
¾ cup shredded Cheddar cheese
6 eggs
¼ cup plus 1 tablespoon buttermilk baking mix, such as Bisquick
¼ cup finely chopped red bell pepper
¼ cup finely chopped shallot
1 can (6 ounces) lump crabmeat, drained well
¾ teaspoon salt
Freshly ground black pepper to taste

Preheat the oven to 325 degrees F. Generously butter a quiche dish, tart pan, or 9-inch pie pan. Coat the pan with the breadcrumbs and sprinkle the cheeses on top. Set aside.

In a mixing bowl, combine the eggs, baking mix, red bell pepper, shallot, crab-meat, salt, and pepper to taste and beat with a whisk or fork until well blended. Pour over the cheese and bake for 35 to 38 minutes. Insert a butter knife into the center of the quiche to make sure the middle is no longer runny. Let stand for 10 minutes. Slice into 6 to 8 slices and serve.

Tip: To drain the crabmeat, empty it into colander or strainer. Press down with your fist to extract the water out of the crab.

Variation: You can substitute ½ cup finely chopped ham for the crabmeat, if desired.

Warm Cinnamon Rolls with Vanilla Icing
Makes about 20 rolls

Nonstick cooking spray
2 cans refrigerated French bread dough, such as Pillsbury Crusty French Loaf
½ cup sugar
2 teaspoons ground cinnamon
3 tablespoons unsalted butter or margarine, softened to room temperature

Vanilla Icing
1 cup powdered sugar
¼ teaspoon vanilla
1 tablespoon milk, plus up to 2 teaspoons more

To make the rolls, preheat the oven to 325 degrees F. Spray two 9-inch round baking pans lightly with cooking spray. Open the packages of dough, and care-fully unroll and flatten each one. In a small mixing bowl, combine the sugar and cinnamon. Spread 1 ½ tablespoons butter or margarine on each dough portion, leaving 1 inch on the long end unbuttered so you can pinch the seam together. Sprinkle half of the sugar and cinnamon mixture on each portion.

Roll one portion of the dough up from a long side. Moisten your fingers with water and seal the seam by pinching the dough together. You will have a long roll. With a piece of dental floss or heavy-duty thread, cut individual rolls by placing the floss under the dough. Crisscross the floss over the dough, pulling quickly to slice off a 1 ½-inch roll. Place cut side up in one of the baking pans, arranging them so the rolls all touch each other. Repeat with the other dough portion and the second pan. Bake for 25 to 28 minutes. Remove from the pan and let cool for 5 minutes.

To make the icing, in a small mixing bowl, combine the powdered sugar, vanilla, and 1 tablespoon milk. Stir. Lift the spoon. If the icing is too stiff and does not drizzle off the spoon, add more milk, 1 teaspoon at a time, until the icing is at a drizzling consistency. Drizzle over the warm cinnamon rolls and serve.

Variation: Sprinkle ¼ cup raisins on top of the sugar and cinnamon before rolling up and cutting the dough.

Tip: Using dental floss to cut the rolls will make a cleaner cut and keep your cinnamon rolls round. If you prefer, use a very sharp knife and shape the slice back into a round roll with your fingers.

Guava Mimosas
Makes 6 to 8 drinks

Sugar for rimming glasses
Guava, mango, or passion fruit juice, chilled (refrigerated section)
1 bottle Champagne, chilled
Small edible flowers, for garnish

Pour some sugar onto a small plate. Moisten the rim of a glass with a bit of juice poured on a napkin. Lightly rub the wet napkin around the rim, turn the glass upside down, and press it down into the sugar to rim the glass. Pour juice into a rimmed glass to fill it halfway. Fill the remainder of the glass with Champagne. Garnish with a small edible flower, such as an orchid. Serve.

Tip: Mimosas are traditionally served in champagne flutes, but if you do not have these, serve them in any nice glassware you have.

51

STEP-BY-STEP CHECKLIST

__2 DAYS BEFORE__	Clean the house, reread the recipes, and make a shopping list.
__1 DAY BEFORE__	Shop.
	Prepare the raspberry vinaigrette; refrigerate.
MORNING OF THE BRUNCH	Set the table, and chill the drinks.
__2 HOURS BEFORE__	Prepare all ingredients for the Smoked Salmon Canapés. Do not assemble yet.
	Prepare the salad, cover, and chill. Take the vinaigrette out of the refrigerator. Do not mix together yet.
__1 HOUR BEFORE__	Prepare the ingredients for the Sweet Crabmeat Quiche. Do not add the egg mixture to the pan yet.
__45 MINUTES BEFORE__	Preheat the oven to 325 degrees F.
	Prepare the Warm Cinnamon Rolls.
	Prepare the Vanilla Icing; set aside.
__30 MINUTES BEFORE__	Pour the egg mixture over the cheeses and bake the quiche.
	Bake the cinnamon rolls.

Assemble the Smoked Salmon Canapés, arrange on a platter, and cover.

Brew a pot of coffee.

5 MINUTES BEFORE   Take the cinnamon rolls out of the oven.

Turn on the music.

AS GUESTS ARRIVE   Take out and cool the quiche; check center for doneness.

Offer Mimosas, juice, or coffee and Smoked Salmon Canapés.

Toss the salad.

Ice the cinnamon rolls.

Slice the quiche.

15 MINUTES AFTER   Serve!

53

OPTIONAL SHORTCUTS

1. Purchase ready-to-bake cinnamon rolls in the refrigerated section of the grocery store.

2. Purchase a jar of real bacon bits instead of frying your own for the spinach salad.

PARTY ETIQUETTE

Giving a toast to the person of honor at *any* special occasion adds a meaningful element to the day. Sometime toward the end of the meal, simply stand up, raise your glass, and announce that you would like to make a toast. You can briefly share what you appreciate most about your mom, a special memory you have of her, or attributes that you admire about her in her presence with your guests. Everyone will in turn raise their glasses and say, "Cheers!" I can guarantee it is something your mother will never forget. It seems as though we always mean to tell people why we admire them, but all too often those things aren't shared. Even if you are not accustomed to speaking in front of others, I encourage you to try. You are in your own home, with those you care about in attendance. Use a 3-by-5-inch card to write down some notes if you need to. Your toast does not need to be long, but say what you want to say to honor her. Don't worry if you think there may be a few tears. If there are, they will be tears of happiness and gratitude. We are alive today. Make the most of every opportunity to build others up and share your generous hospitality.

MISTAKES TO AVOID

Use care when opening a bottle of Champagne. The contents are under pressure and the cork stopper can pop off like a missile. Put a dishtowel over the stopper when opening it, for safety.

TIPS TO ENSURE SUCCESS

The secret to a fantastic salad is to have all of your ingredients well chilled. Never serve your salad at room temperature, because the ingredients will not be crisp. About an hour before you serve, chill your salad plates in the refrigerator for an extra gourmet touch.

CHAPTER 6

FAMILY FIESTA

*E*VERYONE SEEMS TO LOVE MEXICAN FOOD. Made with fresh, simple ingredients, this menu is the one my family requests the most for summer barbecues. The Carne Asada is so tasty that we have actually had guests leave at the end of a fiesta with a stomachache because they couldn't stop eating it. The chips, homemade salsa, and zesty guacamole are classic Mexican recipes. This is a wonderful menu to make in the summertime because tomatoes are at their peak flavor. It is also a great change from burger cookouts. A michelada (pronounced meech-a-lada) is a tart and refreshing beverage made from beer, Clamato or V-8 Juice, lime juice, Worcestershire sauce, and hot sauce. It pairs perfectly with this menu. Paletas are Mexican fruit juice bars that are served for dessert. They come in deliciously different flavors like banana-strawberry, coconut-pineapple, and mandarin orange and can be purchased at a Latin market.

This setup is simple. Purchase a festive piñata from any party store or Latin market and use it as a centerpiece on your table. You can use a striped blanket or poncho for a tablecloth. Or purchase a sombrero and maracas (inexpensive musical instruments) or large crepe paper flowers from a Latin market or party supply store. If you have invited children to your fiesta, fill the piñata with wrapped candy. After the meal, hang it with a rope from a tree, with an adult on the other end of it, controlling it. Have the children line up. Blindfold the first one in line and turn him or her around three times. Give the child a stick or a bat and let him or her whack at the piñata to try to break it. *Caution: Adult supervision is a must; keep others away from the swinging bat!* Try to give each child a turn with a few swings of the bat before the piñata is broken open.

(The adult on the other end will have to creatively move it while the children are trying to hit it.) Once the piñata breaks open, give each child a paper lunch bag and let them rush in and pick up the candy from the ground.

My husband takes a warm flour tortilla and puts in pieces of Carne Asada, rice, beans, and salsa and rolls it up into a burrito. I prefer to take pieces of flour tortilla and scoop up cut-up pieces of steak. I eat my beans, rice with salsa on top, and tomato salad on the side. Any way you eat it, it's mighty good!

This menu is also appropriate for: Father's Day, an adult birthday (purchase a cake), or a neighborhood barbecue.

MENU

Serves 10 to 12

Fresh Salsa and Zesty Guacamole with purchased tortilla chips
Carne Asada
Spanish Rice
Pinto Beans with Bacon
Fresh Tomato Salad with Basil and Panela Cheese
Flour tortillas (purchased)
Paletas (frozen juice bars; purchased)

Drinks

Mexican soda (purchased)
Horchata (rice drink; purchased)
Micheladas
Beer: Corona or Dos Equis

Music Suggestions

Buena Vista Social Club, Gipsy Kings, Gloria Estefan

Fresh Salsa
Makes about 6 cups

6 large tomatoes, finely chopped
5 medium to large jalapeño chiles, seeds removed, finely chopped
2 medium onions or 1 large onion, finely chopped
½ cup chopped cilantro
Juice of 3 limes or 2 large lemons
Bottled hot sauce, such as Cholula or Tapatio, to taste
Salt and freshly ground black pepper to taste

In a large bowl, combine the tomatoes, jalapeños, onions, cilantro, and lime or lemon juice. Add several dashes of hot sauce, depending on how spicy you like it, and salt and pepper to taste (you'll need 1 to 2 teaspoons salt). Put half of the salsa in a serving bowl, cover, and set aside. Do not refrigerate. Put the other half of the salsa in a large bowl and use it for the Zesty Guacamole.

59

Zesty Guacamole
Makes about 6 cups

4 or 5 large, ripe avocados, peeled and pitted
Half of the Fresh Salsa (see previous recipe)
¼ cup fresh lime juice (2 or 3 limes)
Salt and freshly ground black pepper to taste

Using the back of a fork or a potato masher, mash the avocados and add them to the salsa, along with the lime juice. Mix well, adding salt and pepper to taste. Cover and set aside or serve immediately.

Carne Asada
Makes 10 to 12 servings

6 to 7 pounds skirt steak (also called flap meat)
Lawry's Seasoned Salt
Adolph's Meat Tenderizer
Garlic salt
Barbecue spice (spice aisle)
3 or 4 large lemons
1 can beer (any brand)
Flour tortillas, for serving

Light a fire in a charcoal grill, or heat a gas grill to medium-high. The steak should be no more than ¼ inch thick. If the steak you have purchased is thicker, slice it widthwise (horizontally) with a very sharp knife until you have ¼-inch-thick slabs Place a layer of skirt steak on the bottom of a large bowl. Lightly sprinkle all four seasonings on the steak and squeeze some lemon juice over the meat. Turn the meat over and repeat. In addition, sprinkle some beer on this side of the steak. Put your finger over the top of the beer can or bottle so you can just sprinkle it; you do not want to wash all the spices off. Repeat with another layer of steak, seasoning both sides and sprinkling with lemon juice and beer until you have finished all the steak. You will not have used the entire can of beer. Marinate in the refrigerator for no more than 1 hour. Grill until sizzling (3 or 4 minutes per side). Put in a pan and cover with aluminum foil while you are grilling the remainder of the steak. Cut large pieces of grilled steak into serving-size pieces, about 6 by 3 inches, and serve with warm flour tortillas.

Spanish Rice
Makes 10 to 12 servings

¼ cup canola oil
3 cups long-grain rice
5 ½ cups hot water
½ cup tomato sauce
6 teaspoons instant chicken bouillon (soup aisle)
Garlic salt to taste

Heat the oil in a large skillet over medium heat. When the oil is hot, add the rice and cook, stirring constantly, until lightly browned, 5 to 7 minutes. Add the hot water, tomato sauce, chicken bouillon, and garlic salt to taste. Bring to a boil, lower the heat, cover, and simmer until all of the water is absorbed, 25 to 30 minutes.

Pinto Beans with Bacon
Makes 10 to 12 servings

1 pound dried pinto beans
8 ounces salt pork or thick sliced bacon
1 large jalapeño chile
1 to 2 tablespoons garlic salt, plus more if needed
Shredded longhorn or jack cheese for topping (optional)

Put the beans in a colander and rinse in cold water. Transfer them to a large saucepan and cover with water, filling the pot approximately two thirds full. Add the salt pork or bacon, jalapeño, and garlic salt. Bring to a boil, cover, and set the heat to low. Simmer for approximately 3 hours. Check every 30 minutes to make sure the beans are covered in water. If necessary, add a little more water so the beans don't burn. Do not add any water during the last 30 minutes unless the beans are very dry. The water should become thicker and savory and the beans should be juicy, not too dry or too watery. Taste and add more salt, if necessary. Let cool slightly and remove the salt pork or bacon. Either discard it or cut up the lean portion of the bacon and add it back to the beans, discarding the fatty part. Refrigerate until the next day, or serve immediately. Pinto beans are delicious served with shredded longhorn or jack cheese on top.

Fresh Tomato Salad
with Basil and Panela Cheese
Makes 10 to 12 servings

4 large tomatoes, sliced
1 package (12 ounces) Panela cheese (Mexican semisoft cheese)
    or mozzarella, sliced
1 large English (seedless) cucumber, sliced
¼ cup fresh basil, torn into small pieces (produce section)
2 tablespoons extra virgin olive oil
2 tablespoons fresh lime juice
Salt and freshly ground black pepper to taste

On a large platter, arrange a slice of tomato, a slice of cheese, and 2 slices of cucumber. Spread out and repeat until you have used all of the slices. Sprinkle with the basil. Mix together the olive oil and lime juice and drizzle over the salad right before serving. Sprinkle with salt and pepper to taste.

Tip: Never refrigerate tomatoes. It ruins their flavor. The best-flavored tomatoes are ones you either grow yourself or get at a farm stand or farmer's market. Tomatoes in a grocery store are picked before they are completely ripe so they will make it to market before they perish. If you have only tasted tomatoes from a grocery store, you have never really tasted a tomato! If tomatoes from a grocery store are your only choice, purchase vine-ripened tomatoes and put them in a basket on your counter, not in the fridge.

Michelada
Makes 1 drink

Kosher salt for rimming glass
Lemon or lime wedge
¼ cup V-8 or Clamato juice
¼ cup fresh lime or lemon juice
1 or 2 dashes bottled hot sauce, such as Tapatio or Tabasco
Dash of Worcestershire sauce (optional)
1 Tecate or Corona beer

Sprinkle some kosher salt on a saucer. Rub the cut side of a lemon or lime wedge around the rim of a tall glass and dip it in the salt to rim the glass. Add the V-8 or Clamato juice, lime or lemon juice, hot sauce, and Worcestershire sauce, if using, and then pour in the beer. Stir.

Tip: Find kosher salt in the baking aisle next to the regular table salt. This salt is coarser than table salt and is perfect for margaritas and micheladas.

STEP-BY-STEP CHECKLIST

__2 DAYS BEFORE__ Clean the house, reread the recipes, and make a shopping list.

__1 DAY BEFORE__ Shop for all ingredients plus drinks, tortilla chips, 2 dozen flour tortillas, paletas, and a piñata, if desired.

Chill the drinks.

Cook the beans, let cool, cover, and refrigerate.

__MORNING OF THE FIESTA__ Set the table and hang the piñata.

Make the salsa.

__1 HOUR BEFORE__ Rewarm the beans over very low heat, stirring occasionally.

Marinate the Carne Asada.

Prepare the Fresh Tomato Salad with Basil and Panela Cheese.

Mix the oil and lime juice for the salad; set aside.

__30 MINUTES BEFORE__ Light the charcoal or heat the grill.

Make the Spanish Rice.

Make the guacamole.

Set out the salsa, guacamole, tortilla chips, and drinks.

AS GUESTS ARRIVE

Turn on the music.

Grill the Carne Asada.

Put the rice and beans in serving dishes.

Stir and pour the oil and lime juice over the tomato salad; add salt and pepper.

Warm the flour tortillas.

OPTIONAL SHORTCUTS

1. You can purchase guacamole or salsa, but do this only if you absolutely don't have time to make it.

PARTY ETIQUETTE

When inviting guests, give a specific time your fiesta is to start. Allow about 30 minutes for guests to arrive and munch on chips, salsa, and guacamole. When you have decided what time you want to serve the meal (normally 30 to 60 minutes from the start time), serve it regardless of guests that may be running late. You should always serve the guests who have arrived on time. Do not hold up the fiesta for latecomers (except in an emergency situation).

MISTAKES TO AVOID

Skirt steak is an inexpensive cut of meat. If it is not prepared properly, it can be tough, so follow the instructions to assure tender steak. If you have a Latin *carniceria* (meat market) in your area, I recommend buying your skirt steak there. They will have removed the silver skin and extra fat and cut it into thin pieces, perfect for using with tortillas. If you purchase the skirt steak in a grocery store, just be sure to trim all the fat and silver skin off of the meat and cut it widthwise (horizontally) into ¼-inch-thick slabs before marinating.

TIPS TO ENSURE SUCCESS

I warm flour tortillas on my gas stove right over a medium flame for a few seconds on each side. You can warm 2 at a time this way. Or take them out of the packages, wrap them tightly in aluminum foil, and warm in a 350 degree F oven for 10 to 15 minutes. To keep them warm, use a tortilla warmer or put between 2 clean dishtowels and serve immediately.

CHAPTER 7

FOURTH OF JULY BASH

*T*HE FOURTH OF JULY IS AN AWESOME HOLIDAY. People can be as different as night and day, and yet most folks feel patriotism and gratitude for having the privilege to live in this country of abundance. This commonality brings us together on the Fourth. And what fun a backyard barbecue or get-together at a park can be. Good company, good food, and, of course, fireworks!

To welcome your guests, fly the flag by your front door. An American flag is inexpensive to purchase and can be flown on many other occasions. Drugstores and discount stores carry them with poles and hardware in one kit. If you have children attending your bash, have a couple of fun activities for them. Depending on the age, you could set up a badminton, volleyball, or croquet set. You could even set aside a bit of time in the afternoon for some outdoor games. Three-legged race, water balloon toss, egg toss, sack race, or even a family softball game are always fun. If you have an older child or teenager who is artistically gifted, purchase a set of fluorescent poster paints and a paintbrush and let the teen do some fun face-painting for the younger children. As it starts to get dark, children always love sparklers *(adult supervision is always required)*. Try to leave the other fireworks to the pros. Just about every American town or city has a sponsored fireworks event on the evening of the Fourth.

Use the colors red, white, and blue for your tableware. (What else?) You can also purchase small flags at a party supply store and put them in a festive container (like an aluminum galvanized or enamel bucket) in sand or use patriotic banners for decorations on your serving table. Sunflowers in a casual pitcher look great on the table. If you have or can borrow a child's red wagon or even a clean wheelbarrow, fill it with ice and use it as a cooler for drinks.

I have served the Gourmet Hamburger Bar at summer barbecues, and it is always a hit. Yum… hamburgers with all the bling! The blackberry cobbler recipe is my paternal grandmother's. She was born and raised in West Virginia, and the woman can cook! She is 90 years old as I write this. When I went back East to visit her recently, she had prepared a dinner from scratch of roast beef, gravy, potatoes, carrots, bread and jams, and a pie made with berries she had picked herself. Don't let the simple ingredients and easy preparation fool you—the blackberry cobbler is buttery and delicious.

This menu is also appropriate for: Father's Day, a family reunion, or a barbecue picnic at the park.

68

MENU

Serves 10 to 12
Gourmet Hamburger Bar
Tangy Dill Potato Salad
Fruit Salad with Brown Sugar–Lime Dressing
Gran's Blackberry Cobbler with Vanilla Ice Cream

Drinks
French Lemonade
Strawberry Daiquiris

Music Suggestions
Beach Boys
Eagles
Lost Highway by Bon Jovi
Vince Gill
Union Station (bluegrass music)

Gourmet Hamburger Bar
Makes 12 hamburgers

12 slices bacon
1 package (12 ounces) sliced white mushrooms
Salt to taste
1 large red onion, sliced about ¼ inch thick
Olive oil for brushing
2 avocados, peeled, pitted, and sliced
Juice of 1 lemon
4 tomatoes, sliced
12 red leaf lettuce leaves, washed and dried
Sliced sweet and dill pickles
12 slices assorted cheeses (Cheddar, Swiss, jack, pepper jack)
4 pounds lean ground beef
1 ¼ teaspoons kosher salt
½ teaspoon freshly ground black pepper
Nonstick cooking spray
12 gourmet hamburger buns
Ketchup
Mustard
Mayonnaise

Fry the bacon in a skillet until crisp; drain on paper towels. Sauté the mushrooms for 5 minutes in 1 tablespoon of the leftover bacon grease; salt to taste. You may grill some of the onion slices if desired. Brush with olive oil and grill for 10 to 12 minutes, turning once. Prepare the other accompaniments (avocados, tomatoes, lettuce, pickles, and cheese). When slicing the avocados, sprinkle with the juice of 1 lemon. This will prevent them from turning black.

Mix the ground beef with the kosher salt and pepper in a large bowl. Shape into 12 patties about ¾ inch thick. Light a fire in a charcoal grill, or preheat a gas grill to medium. Coat the grill with cooking spray and grill the patties. Turn them once, and do not squish down with the spatula as this will squeeze out all the juice. When cooked to the desired doneness (4 to 5 minutes on each side), put on a serving platter. If making cheeseburgers, put slices of cheese on the burgers and leave on the grill until the cheese is just soft and a little melted, probably no more than 1 minute. Let guests pick their toppings from your gourmet bar.

Tip: Most grocery stores carry a line of gourmet hamburger buns, such as potato, onion, or seven-grain, or you can get fresh French or ciabatta rolls from your bakery. For this meal, definitely do not buy the white enriched bargain buns. The idea is gourmet hamburgers!

Tangy Dill Potato Salad
Makes 10 to 12 servings

2 ½ pounds potatoes (about 8 medium)
2 teaspoons salt for boiling potatoes
4 eggs
3 stalks celery, chopped
½ cup chopped onion
1 cup mayonnaise
½ cup light sour cream
2 teaspoons chopped fresh dill (preferably) or dried dill
1 tablespoon rice vinegar
1 tablespoon Dijon mustard
1 ¼ teaspoons salt
½ teaspoon freshly ground black pepper

Peel the potatoes with a vegetable peeler and cut into 1-inch chunks. Place in a saucepan, and add water to cover and 2 teaspoons salt. Bring to a boil, cover, set the heat to low, and simmer for 18 to 20 minutes, or until just tender when you stick the potatoes with a fork. Do not overcook. Drain in a colander.

Meanwhile, place the eggs in a saucepan and cover with cold water. Bring to a boil over high heat. Set the heat to low and cover. Simmer for 13 minutes. Drain, put the eggs back in the pan, and cover with cold water. When the eggs are cool, drain. Tap each egg on the counter and roll it between the palms of your hands. Peel off the eggshells. Discard the shells and chop the eggs.

In a large bowl, combine the celery, onion, mayonnaise, sour cream, dill, vinegar, mustard, salt, and pepper. Add the potatoes and eggs. Stir well and refrigerate until ready to serve.

Tip: Never leave potato salad unrefrigerated for very long. The eggs and the mayonnaise can spoil fast at room temperature and even faster if left in the sun.

Fruit Salad with Brown Sugar–Lime Dressing
Makes 10 to 12 servings

1 cantaloupe, cleaned and cut into 1-inch chunks
1 pint strawberries, cleaned and sliced
4 cups cubed seedless watermelon (1-inch chunks)
1 cup red seedless grapes
2 cups cubed fresh pineapple (1-inch chunks)

Brown Sugar–Lime Dressing
2 tablespoons fresh lime juice
¼ cup light brown sugar
1 cup vanilla low-fat yogurt

Mix the fruit together in a large bowl. Cover and refrigerate.

To make the dressing, mix the lime juice, brown sugar, and yogurt together in a small bowl. Add to the fruit salad right before serving.

Tip: You may also use a melon baller to scoop out small balls of the cantaloupe and watermelon.

Gran's Blackberry Cobbler
with Vanilla Ice Cream
Makes 10 to 12 servings

¾ cup unsalted butter (1 ½ sticks), cut into 12 pieces
5 cups blackberries, fresh or thawed frozen
2 ¼ cups sugar, divided
2 cups plus 3 tablespoons all-purpose unbleached flour, divided
1 teaspoon salt
4 teaspoons baking powder
2 cups cold water
½ gallon vanilla ice cream

Preheat the oven to 425 degrees F. Melt the butter in a 9-by-13-inch baking pan in the oven. Meanwhile, in a medium bowl, mix the blackberries, ¼ cup of the sugar, and 3 tablespoons of the flour, and pour over the melted butter in the pan. In a separate bowl, combine the remaining 2 cups sugar and 2 cups flour with the salt, baking powder, and water, mixing with a whisk until the lumps are gone. Pour this over the blackberry mixture and butter in the pan and bake for 35 to 40 minutes. Serve warm or at room temperature, with vanilla ice cream.

Variation: For peach cobbler, omit the blackberries, ¼ cup sugar, and 3 table-spoons flour, and add two 16-ounce cans peaches in light syrup. Drain and pour over the butter. Pour the batter over the top and bake.

French Lemonade
Makes 1 gallon

1 gallon water (4 quarts)
Juice of 14 to 16 lemons
1 ½ cups sugar or Splenda (artificial sweetener)
Mint sprigs, for garnish (optional)

French lemonade is not as sweet as typical American lemonade. Use a small hand juicer to juice the lemons and separate the seeds from the juice. Mix the juice with the water and sugar and refrigerate. If you like your lemonade to taste sweeter, add more sugar. Serve over ice. Garnish each serving with a sprig of fresh mint, if desired.

Strawberry Daiquiris
Makes 6 drinks

6 cups sliced strawberries, or 2 packages (12 ounces each) frozen, unsweetened
strawberries
1 can (12 ounces) strawberry nectar (juice aisle)
1 ¼ cups light rum
½ cup fresh lime juice (4 or 5 limes)
½ cup sugar

Combine the strawberries, strawberry nectar, rum, lime juice, and sugar in a blender, and blend until smooth. Pour into a pitcher and serve immediately or store in the freezer until 10 minutes before serving. Stir, pour into glasses, and serve.

STEP-BY-STEP CHECKLIST

2 DAYS BEFORE	Clean the house, reread the recipes, and make a shopping list.
1 DAY BEFORE	Shop.
	Form the hamburgers, cover, and refrigerate.
	Make the French Lemonade; chill.
MORNING OF THE PARTY	Set the table, fly a flag.
	Make the Tangy Dill Potato Salad, cover, and chill.
	Slice all the ingredients for the hamburger bar, cover, and chill.
	Make the blackberry cobbler.
	Make a pitcher of daiquiris; store in the freezer.
	Make the fruit salad and dressing; do not mix them together yet.
1 HOUR BEFORE	Fry the bacon and sauté the mushrooms.
	Set out all ingredients for the hamburger bar.
	Set out drinks with ice.

AS GUESTS ARRIVE   Light charcoal or heat the grill.

Turn on the music.

Toss the fruit salad with the dressing.

Set out all of the food.

Grill the hamburgers, along with some onions, if desired.

OPTIONAL SHORTCUTS

1. You can purchase prepared lemonade in the refrigerated juice or frozen food section of your grocery store.

2. You can purchase a berry pie instead of making the blackberry cobbler.

PARTY ETIQUETTE

As a host it is particularly thoughtful to keep in mind that invited children are guests too. Having a separate table with a couple of crafts for the kids to make and take home can be a lot of fun for them. Have a bucket of sidewalk chalk, play hopscotch or jacks, or be really daring and teach them how to double-dutch jump rope. Boys love basketball, bug hunting, and all types of races.

MISTAKES TO AVOID

Don't pour leftover bacon grease down your sink drain, or it will harden and clog it. Empty it into a coffee cup and later, when it is cooled and hard, scoop it into the trash. That way you will avoid a visit from your friendly neighborhood plumber at premium Fourth of July holiday rates!

TIPS TO ENSURE SUCCESS

Always use a kitchen timer for the correct cooking time. You can purchase one at the grocery store in the baking aisle or in any discount or kitchen store. Learn from others' experience (including my own): Don't make the mistake of thinking you will remember something that is in the oven, getting busy with other things, and all of a sudden smelling smoke. That is not a good sign!

Color Photos of the Recipes

MY FIRST COCKTAIL PARTY

Chapter 1 | Shrimp Ceviche, page 8.

ROMANTIC DINNER FOR TWO

Chapter 2 | Coconut Salmon with Pineapple Salsa, Aromatic Herbed Rice, Broccoli with Lemon and Parmesan, page 15.

DINNER WITH THE IN-LAWS

Chapter 3 | Beef Tenderloin Medallions with Savory Sauce, Baked Potato with Blue Cheese Dressing, Haricots Verts with Garlic and Almonds, page 26.

DINNER WITH THE IN-LAWS

Chapter 3 | Kahlua Fudge Brownie Pie, page 29.

GIRLFRIENDS' TEA

Chapter 4 | page 35.

MOTHER'S DAY BRUNCH

Chapter 5 | Spinach Salad with Raspberry Vinaigrette, Sweet Crabmeat Quiche, Warm Cinnamon Rolls with Vanilla Icing, page 47.

FAMILY FIESTA

Chapter 6 | Fresh Salsa and Zesty Guacamole, Carne Asada, Spanish Rice, Pinto Beans with Bacon, page 59.

FAMILY FIESTA

Chapter 6 | Fresh Tomato Salad with Basil and Panela Cheese, page 62.

FOURTH OF JULY BASH

Chapter 7 | Gran's Blackberry Cobbler, page 72.

LITTLE GIRLS' FRIENDSHIP TEA

Chapter 2 | Lemon Cupcakes with Cream Cheese Filling, page 98.

DINNER WITH CLOSE FRIENDS

Chapter 9 | Chicken Tortilla Soup, page 117.

DINNER WITH CLOSE FRIENDS

Chapter 9 | Egg Custard with Strawberry Nectar, page 119.

GUYS' NIGHT OUT

Chapter 10 | (above) Hot Wings with Blue Cheese Dressing, page 127.
(below) Mega Sandwich, page 129.

MY FIRST THANKSGIVING

Chapter 11 | page 135.

CHRISTMAS SEASON SOCIAL

Chapter 12 | (left to right front row) Cheddar Hash Brown Gratin, Pear, Blue Cheese and Candied Almond Salad with Champagne Vinaigrette, Eggnog, Baked Brie in Crescent Dough, Buttermilk Biscuits with Ham/Turkey, Eggnog Cake with Orange Rum Sauce, page 152.

CHAPTER 8

TWO THEMED CHILDREN'S BIRTHDAY PARTIES

*W*OW, HAVE CHILDREN'S BIRTHDAY PARTIES CHANGED over the years! A child born in the 1950s, '60s, or '70s *might* have had one birthday party during his or her entire childhood. These were pretty simple affairs: usually cake and ice cream, a game or two, and the birthday boy or girl opening their presents. Today, birthday parties have evolved into a billion dollar plus business. Many dads and moms feel that they would be bad parents if their child did not have a party *every* year. So here come the rented bounce houses, carnival rides, petting zoos, professional entertainment, rented facilities, paid party planners, caterers, and, of course, loot bags filled with toys and candy for each guest that attends. It can all be so overwhelming not only to plan but to finance as well.

I always go back to my motivation for entertaining, whether it is for grown-ups or kids. Asking my friends and my child's friends to my home to help me celebrate my youngster's birthday puts the focus on the guests, not necessarily on us. "What?" you say, "but it is all about the birthday child!" Indeed, I have every confidence that my youngster will be blessed as the guests sing "Happy Birthday," he engages in fun activities, and receives gifts. It is his special day, but it is also a chance to teach the importance of being a great host. To reinforce at a young age that guests have gone to the trouble to go to a store to purchase a gift and are setting aside their afternoon to help celebrate teaches him to be "other" minded. Training your kids to be friendly and gracious to guests during the party is a life skill that they will use over and over into adulthood. It is so very important.

So with this in mind, for a child's party, do a few things and strive to do those well. Include your youngster in the planning and preparation. He will have fun and you will have a nice memory of working together. One and a half to two hours is a good amount of time for a younger child's birthday party, two to two and a half hours for an older one. Make sure you put a start time and a finish time on the invitations. Send them out 2 to 3 weeks in advance. Parents are always invited with young children, and older ones (10 and up) actually like to be dropped off at your party by their parents. Always get the parent's phone number in case of an emergency. Make sure you have a helper or two to supervise if the older kids are being dropped off.

Parties usually start with a theme. When our youngest son turned three years old, he was enthralled with firemen and fire trucks, so guess what our theme was? All the party goods had fireman logos, and I decorated his birthday cake in the same motif. His birthday was in June and we had a small yard, but it was big enough to set up a Slip 'n' Slide. The kids all brought their bathing suits and slipped and slid to their heart's content while the parents supervised and visited with each other. We had hot dogs, nachos, cake and ice cream, and a fire truck piñata that all the children had a turn at breaking. Pretty simple by today's standards. But everyone sure seemed to have a lot of fun, including our birthday boy, who received probably five fire trucks that day! And the bonus for the parents in attendance was the long naps their children took when they got home from the party.

Take your cue about the theme from your child's interests. Using a popular cartoon character is fine, but you can also be creative about an interest that your child has and use that as a theme. Sports, teddy bears, everyday heroes such as firemen or policemen, camping, beach activities, dinosaurs, race cars, fairy tales, pirates, or jungle, farm, or ocean creatures can all make fun party themes.

In the pages that follow, I have included one theme with activities and a menu for a little girls' party and one for a little boys' party to get you started.

LITTLE GIRLS' FRIENDSHIP TEA
WITH JEWELRY-MAKING CRAFT

This party is lovely for little girls, ages four and up. You can use it as a birthday party or a fun get-together for your little girl and her friends. Two to three weeks before the party, send the invitations and go on the hunt for some dress-up items. Try a secondhand store or garage sale, or ask an older relative for the following items: hats, boas, costume jewelry, shawls, skirts, or any fun items you might find. Launder them as needed. As the girls arrive, have them dress up over their clothes, and have a full-length mirror so they can see themselves. If you have smaller table, set that the same as for the "Girlfriends' Tea" (Chapter 4). Or if you have a child's tea set, you can use that. If not, use what you have. Before you serve the tea, have an area designated for a craft that the girls can make and take home. Most little girls love jewelry, so visit your local craft store. Have an assortment of colorful beads and cord so they can make necklaces or bracelets. *Adult supervision is required when working with small beads.* If the girls are a little older, you could buy plain straw hats at a craft store and have lots of silk flowers, ribbons, buttons, and decorations for the girls to attach. You will need a glue gun that an adult should help with because the glue gets hot. They can wear their hats at the tea and then take them home. You can also play a game or two if time permits. If the girls are elementary school age, you can even try the Victorian parlor game described in Chapter 4.

Use teacups and little plates for the food. Let them add their own sugar cubes to their tea. Talk to them about how proper ladies always took tea every afternoon in days gone by. Put the emphasis on friendship and explain to them that a good friend is kind, compassionate, and loyal. Make it fun, and take advantage of the opportunity you have to build each little girl up. Put a single candle in the birthday girl's cupcake and light it as everyone sings "Happy Birthday." Rather than giving the usual loot bag to the guests, the girls can either take their jewelry craft home or the decorated hat craft.

MENU

Serves 6 to 8
Cucumber and Cream Cheese Sandwiches
Peanut Butter and Honey Crème Sandwiches
Chocolate-Drizzled Strawberries
Lemon Cupcakes with Cream Cheese Filling
Passion Fruit Tea

Cucumber and Cream Cheese Sandwiches

See the recipe in Chapter 4, "Girlfriends' Tea," page 37. Cut the recipe in half.

Peanut Butter
and Honey Crème Sandwiches
Makes about 20 small sandwiches

½ loaf white or wheat bread
Creamy-style peanut butter
Spun or whipped honey

Spread peanut butter and honey crème on one side of half of the slices of bread. Top with the remaining slices and cut into sandwiches with a small heart-shaped cookie cutter. Arrange on a pretty tray. (You may also cut the sandwiches into small triangles if you do not have a cookie cutter.)

Note: Honey is not recommended for children under 1 year of age. Also, as a precaution, check with the parents to make sure none of the girls has a peanut allergy.

Chocolate-Drizzled Strawberries
Makes 12 strawberries

1 dozen large fresh strawberries
1 cup semisweet chocolate chips
1 tablespoon unsalted butter

Wash and dry the strawberries. Lay them out on wax paper. Melt the chocolate chips and butter in a microwave-safe bowl for 30 to 45 seconds. Stir and microwave for 15 more seconds if necessary, until all of the chocolate is melted. Stir until smooth. Using a spoon, drizzle the chocolate in a zigzag pattern across

97

each strawberry, working quickly before the chocolate hardens, until all of the strawberries have drizzled chocolate on top. Refrigerate until ready to use.

Lemon Cupcakes with Cream Cheese Filling
Makes about 18 cupcakes

1 ½ packages (8 ounces each) reduced-fat cream cheese, softened
½ cup powdered sugar
1 package (18 to 19 ounces) lemon cake mix, plus the ingredients listed on the
*   box to prepare the cupcakes*
1 can ready-to-use lemon frosting, such as Pillsbury
Sprinkles or candy flowers

Preheat the oven to 350 degrees F. Line a muffin pan with paper cupcake liners.

In a medium mixing bowl, beat the cream cheese and powdered sugar with an electric mixer until fluffy (about 1 minute). Set aside.

In a large mixing bowl, combine the cake mix plus the ingredients listed and prepare the cake batter according to the directions on the box.

Pour 2 tablespoons cake batter into the bottom of each cupcake liner. Pour 2 teaspoons cream cheese mixture into each cupcake liner. Top with 2 more tablespoons of cake batter in each cupcake liner.

Bake for 22 to 24 minutes. Cool completely. Frost with purchased frosting and cover each cupcake with sprinkles or candy flowers.

Passion Fruit Tea

4 cups boiling water for each teapot
1 box Tazo Passionfruit tea or any herbal fruit tea with no caffeine

Fill a teapot with the boiling water. Add 2 or 3 teabags and steep for 4 to 5 minutes. Take out the teabags and let the tea cool for an additional 2 to 3 minutes.

STEP-BY-STEP CHECKLIST

2 WEEKS BEFORE	Send invitations.
1 WEEK BEFORE	Pick up all your dress-up items, jewelry, or hat craft items.
2 DAYS BEFORE	Reread the recipes and make a shopping list.
	Launder dress-up items as needed.
1 DAY BEFORE	Shop.
	Set up the jewelry-making or hat craft table.
	Make the lemon cupcakes, cover tightly, and refrigerate. Do not frost.
MORNING OF THE PARTY	Set the table.
	Organize the dress-up items.
	Prepare the strawberries.
	Take the cupcakes out of the fridge; frost.
1 HOUR BEFORE	Prepare the cucumber and cream cheese sandwiches.
	Prepare the peanut butter and honey crème sandwiches.
	Set out all of the food, covered with plastic wrap.

AS THE GIRLS ARRIVE

Time for dress-up.

Jewelry-making craft or decorated hat craft.

Victorian parlor game or other game.

Make tea and serve with sandwiches and strawberries.

Serve cupcakes and sing "Happy Birthday."

Open presents.

OPTIONAL SHORTCUTS

1. Purchase cupcakes from a bakery or grocery store if time is really tight.

2. Many craft stores carry craft kits specifically for children's parties, with everything in one package for several children to make something fun. This is a great, inexpensive idea to make your life a little easier.

3. Instead of hunting for dress-up items, visit your local craft store. Many carry inexpensive feather boas for little girls. Ooh-la-la!

MISTAKES TO AVOID

When serving the tea, be especially careful that it is warm and not too hot for the girls.

PARTY ETIQUETTE

Use the teatime to teach the girls how to be a wonderful friend, and make a point to set an example by using good manners with them, such as saying "please" and "thank you."

TIPS TO ENSURE SUCCESS

One way to save time is to shop on the Internet. OrientalTrading.com is one company that carries all of the items needed for both parties, and you can shop from the comfort of your home!

LITTLE BOYS' TRICYCLE OLYMPICS PARTY

This party is designed for boys, ages four to eight. Most little boys are naturally competitive. They like a challenge! It is a God-given drive and will serve them later in life as they embark on a career. It is a good thing to nurture this trait as long as it is balanced by teaching fair play and good sportsmanship. Little boys would love to get a birthday party invitation where they can bring their own tricycles and bicycles to compete in some fun games. When you send the invitations, make sure you tell them that, in addition to bringing their bikes, they must bring a helmet to participate in the races. It is also a good idea to bring elbow and knee pads for extra protection. If you have a couple of spare bikes and helmets, you can make them available to boys who want to attend but might not have the equipment.

This party will work out well if you have a long driveway or a large concrete patio. Make sure you have two adults to help supervise the boys. Give the boys some free time as they arrive to ride their bikes. Then start the Olympics! Have a 15-yard (or more) dash with a ribbon finish line. If you don't have enough room for all the boys to race at once, break it up into two different races, by age. You can use small orange cones to mark the racing area or use sidewalk chalk to draw the racetrack out on your driveway. A slalom course where they have to negotiate turns around the cones is fun and challenging. If the boys are younger, send just one child through the course at a time and time him with a stopwatch. Otherwise, that irresistible competitive nature may come out, and the race could end up more like a demolition derby than the dignified Olympics! You can also divide the partygoers into teams of three and have a relay race. As the first boy crosses the finish line, you tell the next boy to go, and when he gets to the finish line, your adult helper tells the last boy to go. Don't have a baton to hand off, as in a real relay race, because the boys need to have both hands on the handlebars.

Purchase small trophies or medals for the different events from a party supply store or online, with awards for first, second, and third place. Talk to the boys before the races about good sportsmanship, and emphasize having fun. Encourage them to be happy for the winners and to congratulate them by shaking their hand. If there is a boy or two in attendance whose strength is not athletics, congratulate them on their effort. Award a medal for best effort or best sportsmanship if, in fact, he shows good sportsmanship. You could even have the winners put their hands over their heart when they receive their trophy or medal and play the national anthem. Offer four or five different races.

While one group is racing, have one of the other adults take three or four boys to the kitchen to make their own custom pizzas. This can also be done when they have free bike-riding time at the beginning of the party. The boys will love being in control of choosing all their own pizza toppings. You will have the individual dough prepared, with toppings set out that the boys can choose. The adult can then bake the pizzas and rotate with the next group of boys while the others are racing. When the racing and awards ceremony is over, the custom pizzas will be ready for the boys to eat. Then on to singing "Happy Birthday" and opening presents!

MENU

Serves 6 to 8
Pizza Bar
Grapes and watermelon slices
Chocolate Cupcakes
Sparkling Punch

Pizza Bar
Makes 8 individual pizzas

Crust
8 cups all-purpose unbleached flour
2 tablespoons plus 2 teaspoons baking powder
4 teaspoons salt
2 ⅔ cups milk
1 cup canola oil
Olive oil for brushing crusts

Toppings
3 cups spaghetti or pizza sauce (purchased)
4 cups shredded mozzarella cheese
2 cups shredded Cheddar cheese
2 cups sliced pepperoni
1 pound sausage meat, cooked
2 cups cubed ham
2 cups drained pineapple tidbits
2 cups chopped tomato

To make the crust, mix together the flour, baking powder, and salt in a large bowl. Add the milk and canola oil and stir together until a dough forms, Gather the dough in your hands and shape it into a ball. With the heels of your hands, knead the dough on a floured countertop about 10 times, until smooth. Divide the dough into 8 small balls.

Roll each ball into a flat, 6-inch circle with a rolling pin. Place the crusts on a baking sheet, pinch the edges up, and brush with a little olive oil. Repeat with all the dough circles, cover with plastic wrap, and refrigerate until ready for use. (You can fit 2 crusts on each baking sheet.)

To assemble, preheat the oven to 425 degrees F. Take the crusts from the refrigerator, spread each with sauce, and let the children pick toppings and sprinkle them on their pizza. Have a pen and paper ready to write down the child's name and a number to help you keep track so you can give them the right pizza after it is baked. Bake 4 pizzas at a time (2 per baking sheet) for 12 to 15 minutes.

Tip: Feel free to choose any other toppings you think the boys will like.

Chocolate Cupcakes
Makes about 18 cupcakes

1 package (18 to 19 ounces) devil's food cake mix
1 package (3.9 ounces) instant chocolate fudge pudding and pie filling mix
3 eggs
1 ⅓ cups water
½ cup canola oil
1 can ready-to-use chocolate frosting, such as Pillsbury
Sprinkles

Preheat the oven to 350 degrees F. Line a muffin pan with paper cupcake liners. In a large mixing bowl, combine the cake mix, pudding mix, eggs, water, and oil and beat with an electric mixer on medium speed for about 1 minute or until well mixed.

Fill paper liners two thirds full with cake batter. Bake for 22 to 24 minutes. Cool completely. Frost with purchased frosting and sprinkle with candy sprinkles.

Sparkling Punch
Makes about 3 quarts

2 quarts cranberry juice or any other fruit juice
1 liter ginger ale or lemon-lime soda

Mix the juice and soda together right before serving.

STEP-BY-STEP CHECKLIST

2 TO 3 WEEKS BEFORE   Send invitations.

1 WEEK BEFORE   Plan your races.

Pick up small orange cones or sidewalk chalk.

Purchase medals or trophies for first, second, and third place for the number of races you are having.

2 DAYS BEFORE   Reread recipes and make a shopping list.

Shop (don't forget the grapes and watermelon).

1 DAY BEFORE   Make the chocolate cupcakes, cover, and refrigerate. Do not frost.

MORNING OF THE PARTY   Set up racing courses and a medal or trophy table.

Set the table.

Prepare the pizza dough, cover, and refrigerate.

Cook the sausage and cut up all the pizza toppings; cover and refrigerate.

Wash the grapes and cut up the watermelon; cover and refrigerate.

Chill the punch ingredients.

Frost the cupcakes.

AS GUESTS ARRIVE

Free bike-riding time or start the races.

Have one group of three or four children prepare their pizzas with another adult (it will take approximately 30 minutes to bake all the pizzas).

DURING THE PARTY

Last group of children prepare their pizzas.

While the last pizzas are baking, have the awards ceremony.

Mix the punch.

Eat lunch.

Serve cupcakes and sing "Happy Birthday."

Open presents.

OPTIONAL SHORTCUTS

1. You can use purchased pizza dough from the refrigerated section of the grocery store instead of making it from scratch, if desired.

2. Purchase prepared cupcakes from a bakery or grocery store.

PARTY ETIQUETTE

What is the proper way to thank someone for a gift? For formal affairs such as weddings and showers, thank-you notes are a *must*. This acknowledges to the person who purchased the gift that first of all, you received it; second, that you know that particular gift was from them; and third, that you appreciated it. Generally, a verbal thank-you is sufficient for a child's birthday party, but make sure that your child takes the time to thank each child who has brought him a gift. If Grandpa and Grandma or anyone else has sent a gift, a thank-you note is always appreciated. If your child does not write yet, have him color a picture and then write "thank you" across the top. At the very least, you should have your child call to thank someone who was not in attendance at the party but sent a gift. Thank-yous should never be neglected when someone is kind enough to purchase a gift.

MISTAKES TO AVOID

It is *always* improper to either ask for money for a gift or ask for donations to help pay for the event from your guests. A gift, by its very definition, is not an obligation and should not be dictated by the recipient. It is totally up to the person purchasing the gift to decide what the gift will be. Of course, the purchaser desires to give a gift that the recipient will like and can use. Teaching your child to graciously accept and show thanks for any gifts received honors the person who was thoughtful enough to take the time and expense to purchase it for the recipient.

TIPS TO ENSURE SUCCESS

Naughty children… every host's worst fear when entertaining. If you have a child in attendance who is acting unacceptably (hitting other children, jumping on the couch, chasing the dog, etc.) the first choice is for the parent(s) to handle correction. Feel free to speak to the child about it if the parent is not right there to correct him or is distracted. Get down to his level and tell him calmly but firmly that his behavior is not acceptable and he must stop. If the child does not respond, calmly and privately tell the parent that you have already spoken to the child and that he might hurt himself or others and has not responded to your request. Ask the parent courteously if he or she would be kind enough to assist you by dealing with the situation. Most parents will be happy to comply.

111

CHAPTER 9

DINNER PARTY WITH CLOSE FRIENDS

OST PEOPLE COUNT THEMSELVES VERY BLESSED to have a few close friends. You can encourage one another, you can share your burdens with each other, and you can relax and be yourself when you are with them, knowing that they care for you. What better way to show your love and appreciation for them than to have them into your home for a relaxing evening that includes a delicious meal? Not to mention sharing your effervescent personality!

This menu is all prepared in advance, so you will be able to be just as relaxed and ready to have fun as your friends will be. Some people like to visit and converse all evening, and some like to play cards or board games or even watch a good movie together later in the evening. Whatever your style, this menu will satisfy your group. Serve your guests a glass of wine or a Lemon Drop Martini. Next, serve the crisp Southwest Caesar Salad, dense and delicious cornbread with honey butter, and the zesty Chicken Tortilla Soup. The dessert is a light and elegant egg custard with a sauce of strawberry nectar. Serve this meal buffet style so your friends can add their own toppings of cheese, avocado, cilantro, lime, and fresh fried tortilla chips to their soup. You may either prepare the soup the day before your dinner or the morning of the party. It will taste great either way.

This menu is also appropriate for: Dinner with business associates, an adult birthday party (purchase a birthday cake), or a co-ed bridal shower.

MENU

Serves 6 to 8
Southwest Caesar Salad
Cornbread with Honey Butter
Chicken Tortilla Soup
Egg Custard with Strawberry Nectar

Drinks
Lemon Drop Martinis
Wines: pinot noir or syrah

Music Suggestions
Trav'lin' Light by Queen Latifah
Exclusive by Chris Brown

Southwest Caesar Salad

Dressing
½ cup olive oil, divided
2 teaspoons Worcestershire sauce
1 tablespoon sherry wine vinegar
Grated zest of 1 lime
1 small serrano chile, seeded and chopped
1 tablespoon mayonnaise
¼ teaspoon salt

Salad
3 heads romaine lettuce, or 2 bags (10 ounces each) prepared chopped romaine
½ cup chopped cilantro
¾ cup grated Cotija Mexican cheese or Parmesan cheese
1 cup purchased croutons

To make the dressing, put ¼ cup of the olive oil in a blender or food processor with the Worcestershire sauce, vinegar, lime zest, chile, mayonnaise, and salt. Thoroughly blend together. Very slowly pour in the remaining ¼ cup olive oil while blending on low speed. Taste and, if necessary, add more salt.

To make the salad, if using heads of romaine, remove the outer leaves and discard. Wash and dry the romaine and chop coarsely. Place in a large salad bowl. Add the cilantro and cheese. Cover and refrigerate until ready to serve.

Right before serving, add the croutons to the salad. Shake or whisk the dressing well and toss about half to three fourths of the salad dressing with the salad. Serve immediately, alongside the cornbread and honey butter.

Cornbread with Honey Butter
Makes about 9 pieces

4 tablespoons unsalted butter (½ stick)
1 ½ cups yellow cornmeal
¼ cup all-purpose unbleached flour
1 teaspoon baking soda
2 tablespoons sugar
1 teaspoon salt
2 cups buttermilk
1 egg, slightly beaten

Honey Butter
½ cup salted butter (1 stick), softened to room temperature
3 tablespoons honey

To make the cornbread, preheat the oven to 425 degrees F. Melt the butter in an 8-by-8-inch glass pan in the microwave for 45 to 60 seconds, or, if using a metal pan, melt the butter in the pan in the oven as it heats. Stir until melted. Mix the dry ingredients together in a large bowl. Stir in the buttermilk, then stir in the beaten egg. Pour in the melted butter from the pan and mix well. Pour the batter into the baking pan and bake for 25 minutes.

To make the honey butter, mix together the butter and honey. Serve with the cornbread.

Tip: If you do not have buttermilk, mix together 2 cups whole milk and 2 tablespoons lemon juice or white vinegar. Let sit for 5 minutes before using.

Chicken Tortilla Soup
Makes 6 to 8 servings

1 whole rotisserie chicken (available at most grocery stores), or Basic Chicken, page 164

3 quarts chicken broth (soup aisle)

½ teaspoon crushed red pepper flakes

1 tablespoon salt

Freshly ground black pepper to taste

2 tablespoons olive oil

2 white onions, chopped

2 jalapeño chiles, seeded and chopped

4 cloves garlic, finely chopped

1 bay leaf

1 ½ teaspoons dried oregano

3 large tomatoes, chopped

2 dozen corn tortillas

1 ½ cups canola oil, plus more if needed

1 avocado

1 tablespoon fresh lime juice

Shredded longhorn Cheddar or jack cheese

2 limes, quartered

¼ cup chopped cilantro

Skin, bone, and shred the chicken meat; store in an airtight container in the refrigerator until ready to use. Pour the chicken broth into a large soup pot. Add the crushed red pepper flakes, salt, and pepper to taste and turn the heat to medium. In a medium frying pan, heat the olive oil over medium heat and sauté the onions, jalapeños, garlic, bay leaf, and oregano, stirring constantly, for 4 to 5 minutes, until the onions are transparent. Add the tomatoes and cook for 2 or 3 minutes more. Carefully add this mixture to the chicken broth and simmer for a total of 20 to 30 minutes. After 10 minutes, ladle out about 2 cups of the broth mixture into a medium bowl and let cool slightly; you'll use this to thicken the soup. Continue to simmer the remaining broth.

While the soup is simmering, cut the corn tortillas into quarters. Heat the canola oil in a large frying pan over medium-high heat. Fry the tortilla quarters in the hot oil, turning once, until very crisp. Drain on paper towels. Sprinkle lightly with salt. Watch the heat and turn it down to medium if necessary. Continue until all the tortilla quarters are fried. Add more oil to the pan if necessary.

Pour 1 cup of the reserved, cooled chicken broth into a blender. Crush about 10 of the tortilla quarters into the broth and blend carefully to thicken. Add this thickened mixture to the soup pot to thicken the soup. Repeat with 10 more tortilla quarters and the last cup of reserved broth, and add to the soup pot. Simmer for an additional 10 to 15 minutes. Keep the remaining fried tortilla quarters warm in the oven (set at 180 degrees F) and serve with the soup. Chop the avocado. Squeeze a tablespoon of lime juice over the avocado and stir to prevent it from turning black. Microwave the shredded chicken for 2 to 3 minutes.

118

To serve, ladle some soup broth into an individual bowl. Add some warm shredded chicken. Let your guests sprinkle shredded cheese on top, squeeze fresh lime juice into the soup, and add chopped avocado, cilantro, and fried tortilla quarters.

Tip: When chopping jalapeños, cut off the stem first and then cut the pepper in half lengthwise. With a small knife, cut out the seeds and white ribs and discard. Cut the pepper lengthwise into strips about ⅛ inch wide. Turn and chop the strips widthwise to end up with finely chopped pepper. After you are finished, be sure to wash your hands with soap and warm water, especially under your nails. If you forget to wash your hands and you touch your eye later, it will burn from the pepper you have left on your hands.

Egg Custard with Strawberry Nectar
Makes 8 servings

6 eggs, beaten
1 ½ cups milk
1 ½ cups half-and-half
⅔ cup sugar
2 teaspoons vanilla
Nonstick cooking spray
¼ teaspoon ground nutmeg
1 can (8 ounces) Kern's strawberry nectar or other fruit nectar
1 small can whipped cream (optional)
8 small strawberries, for garnish (optional)

Special Equipment
Eight 6-ounce ramekins or custard cups

119

Preheat the oven to 325 degrees F. In a medium mixing bowl, beat the eggs, milk, half-and-half, sugar, and vanilla well with a whisk. Have ready eight 6-ounce ramekins or custard cups (you can also use coffee cups that are oven-safe). Spray the bottom of each ramekin lightly with cooking spray. Divide the custard mixture evenly among the ramekins and sprinkle with a bit of ground nutmeg. Place the ramekins into a 9-by-13-inch baking pan. Carefully set the pan in the oven and pour boiling water into the pan, around the ramekins, so the water is about 1 inch deep. This method will steam the custard. Close the oven door and cook for 45 to 50 minutes, or until a butter knife inserted in the center of one of the custards comes out clean. If they are still liquid in the middle, bake for 5 more minutes and check again. Repeat if necessary until the knife comes out clean. Cool, cover, and refrigerate until ready to serve.

To serve, slide a butter knife around the edge of the ramekin and invert it into a dessert bowl to release the custard. Pour 2 to 3 tablespoons of the strawberry nectar on top. Finish with a small bit of whipped cream on top and a fresh strawberry for garnish, if desired. You may also serve the custards in their cups, with the strawberry nectar alongside in a small gravy boat so guests can pour their own.

Tip: Nonstick cooking spray is basically oil in a spray can. It is usually found in the baking section of the grocery store. Spraying the ramekins lightly will allow the custards to slip out for easier serving.

Lemon Drop Martini
Makes 1 martini

Sugar for rimming glass
Lemon wedge
¼ cup lemon-flavored vodka
3 tablespoons bottled sweet-and-sour mix (liquor aisle or liquor store)
2 tablespoons Cointreau (French orange liqueur)
2 tablespoons fresh lemon juice

Pour some sugar onto a small plate. Rub the rim of the martini glass with the cut edge of the lemon wedge. Turn the glass upside down and twist the rim lightly in the sugar. Pour the vodka, sweet-and-sour mix, Cointreau, and lemon juice into a cocktail shaker filled with ice and shake. Strain the chilled mixture into the glass, leaving the ice in the shaker.

STEP-BY-STEP CHECKLIST

__2 DAYS BEFORE__   Clean the house, reread the recipes, and make a shopping list.

__1 DAY BEFORE__   Shop.

Make the custard, cool, cover, and refrigerate.

Shred the chicken; refrigerate in an airtight container.

Make the honey butter; cover and refrigerate.

Optional: If you wish, you can make the soup today, cool, cover, and chill. Then fry the tortillas tomorrow and follow the recipe directions to thicken the soup with the fried tortillas.

121

__MORNING OF THE PARTY__   Make the soup, cover, and refrigerate.

Put the leftover tortilla quarters in a zipper-lock bag.

Make the salad dressing.

Prepare the salad (do not mix in the croutons or dressing), cover, and refrigerate.

Set the table.

__1 HOUR BEFORE__   Prepare and bake the cornbread.

Warm the soup on low.

Quarter the limes and chop the cilantro.

Chop the avocado and sprinkle with lime juice.

Place the limes, cilantro, shredded cheese, and avocado in small bowls or on a lazy Susan for serving.

Take the honey butter out of the refrigerator.

15 MINUTES BEFORE Warm the fried tortilla quarters on a baking sheet in the oven at 180 degrees F.

Unmold the custards into dessert bowls and keep in the refrigerator until ready to serve.

Turn on the music, and light candles, if using.

AS GUESTS ARRIVE Serve the drinks.

Serve the salad, cornbread, and honey butter.

Second course: Serve the tortilla soup with the fried tortillas and other toppings.

SOMETIME DURING THE EVENING Serve the Egg Custard with Strawberry Nectar.

OPTIONAL SHORTCUTS

If you absolutely do not have time to fry the tortillas, you could purchase them, but fresh ones add so much to the meal, so do try to fry your own.

PARTY ETIQUETTE

A gentleman should seat a female at a dinner party by holding her chair and seating her on his right.

MISTAKES TO AVOID

Be cautious when frying tortillas in hot oil. If the oil starts to smoke, it is too hot. Turn the heat down. Use an apron if you have one, so the oil will not spatter on your clothing.

123

TIPS TO ENSURE SUCCESS

Whenever you are following a recipe, take all your ingredients out of the cupboard and refrigerator before you do any other preparation. Chop or grate the ingredients as listed. After all your ingredients are ready, proceed with the additional instructions. Don't try to start by mixing ingredients in bowls when you don't have all ingredients chopped or grated. You will have much better success with your recipes if you follow this tip.

CHAPTER 10

GUYS' NIGHT OUT

*W*HETHER IT IS POKER, SUPERBOWL, NASCAR racing, or boxing —you name it and guys like to get together to play it or watch it. Can you blame them? The agenda includes some friendly ribbing, the chance to win a buddy's money, cheering on the team favorite, and, of course, consuming tasty food with lots of meat! Don't even try to serve a salad at one of these get-togethers. Believe me, I have raised three men who know what their fellow gender mates like, and their input has guided the menu selection here.

Hot wings have not waned in popularity over the years, and the spicy, finger-licking sauce on the wings invites a dip in the cool blue cheese dressing. The Mega Sandwich is made with a large, round loaf of bread, three layers high, stuffed with ingredients dominated by meat. The Chili Boats are a delicious mix of flavor, spice, and crunch. Serve everything with cold beer and plenty of napkins. Hefeweizen is a beer made from wheat and barley and tastes best poured into a chilled glass with a generous slice of lemon or orange. A Black & Tan is made with two types of beer, a dark Guinness and a light Bass Ale. If you would like a wider selection of munchies, feel free to offer some purchased finger food, such as prepared egg rolls, taquitos, pot stickers, California rolls, spicy tuna rolls, or any other food you think the guys will enjoy. Serve the easy-to-eat cheesecake brownie bars as a sweet ending to the meal. Most items are made in advance, and the last thing to do is warm the chili and the Mega Sandwich. And if you are worried about the apparent lack of vegetables on the menu, take heart: The guys might consume one or two of the celery or carrot sticks served with the hot wings.

This menu is also appropriate for: Father's Day (Add the Southwest Caesar Salad from Chapter 9), an adult male birthday party (purchase a birthday cake), or a tailgate party (prepare all menu items at home; place the chili in large thermoses and wrap the sandwich and wings tightly in heavy-duty foil for transporting to the party).

MENU

Serves 8

Hot Wings with Blue Cheese Dressing

Chili Boats with All the Fixin's

The Mega Sandwich

Smoked almonds (purchased)

Easy Cheesecake Brownies

Drinks

Beer: Pyramid Hefeweizen

Black & Tans

Music

2008 Grammy Nominees

Contemporary mix CD (with a variety of hip-hop, rock, etc.)

Hot Wings with Blue Cheese Dressing
Makes 50 to 60 wings

Wing Sauce
4 tablespoons unsalted butter (½ stick)
¼ cup brown sugar
¼ cup bottled hot sauce, such as Frank's, Tabasco, or Tapatio
½ bottle purchased hot wing sauce, such as Frank's

Hot Wings
25 to 30 chicken wings
1 cup all-purpose unbleached flour
½ teaspoon salt
1 teaspoon ground cayenne pepper
Nonstick cooking spray
8 celery stalks, cleaned and cut into 4- to 6-inch pieces
8 carrots, cleaned and cut into 4- to 6-inch pieces

Blue Cheese Dressing
Double recipe of Blue Cheese Dressing, page 27

To make the wing sauce, melt the butter in a small bowl in the microwave for 30 seconds. Add the brown sugar, hot sauce, and hot wing sauce; stir to combine.

To make the wings, preheat the oven to 400 degrees F. Spread out a chicken wing; it will have 3 parts. At the joint, cut off the wing tip, using kitchen scissors or a sharp knife, and discard. Bend the remaining wing into 2 pieces at the joint and cut through to have 2 separate pieces. Repeat with the remaining wings. Wash and dry the chicken pieces. In a zipper-lock bag, combine the flour, salt, and cayenne pepper. Put about 5 wings at a time into the bag, and shake to coat. Put the floured wings on a baking sheet sprayed with cooking spray. Bake for 35 minutes, and then brush generously with wing sauce. Return to the oven and bake for 8 to 10 minutes longer. Remove from the oven, turn the wings over, and brush the other side generously with sauce. Bake for 5 more minutes. Slather with more sauce and serve immediately with the celery and carrot sticks and the blue cheese dressing.

Chili Boats with All the Fixin's
Serves 8

2 tablespoons vegetable oil
2 pounds ground boneless beef chuck
1 large white onion, chopped
1 green bell pepper, seeds removed, chopped
4 cloves garlic, chopped
1 can (28 ounces) crushed tomatoes
1 tablespoon ground cumin
1 ½ tablespoons dried oregano
¼ cup chili powder
¼ to ½ teaspoon ground cayenne pepper
2 cups (one 14-ounce can) beef broth (soup aisle)
1 tablespoon salt, plus more to taste
2 cans (15 ounces each) small red beans (pinquitos) or pinto beans
Freshly ground black pepper
1 bag (9 ¾ ounces) Fritos corn chips

Toppings
3 cups shredded Cheddar cheese
2 cups sour cream
2 limes, cut into wedges
3 large jalapeño chiles, sliced
½ cup chopped cilantro

In a large Dutch oven or pot, heat the vegetable oil and brown the ground chuck. Drain the fat from the meat by carefully holding the lid with potholders slightly askew and pouring the fat into a coffee cup. (Don't pour it down the sink.) Add the onion and green pepper and cook, stirring, for 4 to 5 minutes. Add the garlic and cook for 1 minute more. Stir in the tomatoes, cumin, oregano, chili powder, cayenne pepper, beef broth, and 1 tablespoon salt. Simmer for 1 hour over low heat. Add the beans and salt and pepper to taste and simmer for 5 minutes.

To serve, put a handful of Fritos in the bottom of a bowl. Top with a ladleful of chili and let guests add their own toppings.

Tip: If you can't remember when you purchased your bottled spices, it is time to throw them out and purchase new ones. Most spices lose their flavor after a few months. New ones will give the chili the best flavor.

The Mega Sandwich
Makes 8 servings

8 slices bacon
8-inch round loaf sourdough bread, unsliced
Mustard
Horseradish (optional)
12 ounces thinly sliced cooked roast beef
5 slices colby cheese
Mayonnaise
8 ounces thinly sliced cooked turkey breast
4 slices pepper jack cheese
1 medium tomato, sliced
1 small onion, sliced (optional)
Salt and freshly ground black pepper to taste
1 tablespoon unsalted butter, melted
Garlic powder

Preheat the oven to 375 degrees F. Fry the bacon slices. Drain on a paper towel and set aside. Slice the bread horizontally into 4 even layers. Spread the bottom layer with mustard and/or horseradish, and top with the roast beef and colby cheese. Place the next slice of bread on top, spread with mayonnaise, and add the turkey breast, bacon, and pepper jack cheese. Place the third slice of bread on top, spread lightly with mayonnaise, and top with tomato and onion slices. Salt and pepper the tomato slices. Top with the last slice of bread. Brush the top of the bread with the melted butter, and sprinkle lightly with garlic powder. Place the sandwich on a baking sheet, cover loosely with foil, and bake for 15 to 20 minutes. Cut into wedges and serve.

Easy Cheesecake Brownies
Makes about 24 brownies

1 package (20.5 ounces) brownie mix, plus the ingredients listed on the box to prepare the brownies
Nonstick cooking spray

Cheesecake Topping
1 package (8 ounces) reduced-fat cream cheese, softened to room temperature
½ cup sugar
2 eggs
2 tablespoons fresh lemon juice
1 cup milk chocolate chips (optional)

Preheat the oven to 350 degrees F. Prepare the brownie batter according to the package directions. Spray a 9-by-13-inch baking pan with cooking spray. Spread the brownie mixture in the pan and partially bake for 15 minutes.

To make the cheesecake topping, mix the cream cheese, sugar, eggs, and lemon juice together in a medium bowl and carefully spread on top of the partially baked brownie. Continue baking for 20 minutes, or until a toothpick inserted in the middle comes out clean. Top with the chocolate chips, if desired. Cool completely and cut into bars.

Beer

Hefeweizen
One 12-pack Pyramid Hefeweizen
3 oranges
3 lemons

Black & Tans
One 6-pack Guinness
One 6-pack Bass Ale

To serve the Hefeweizen, pour into a chilled glass and add a generous slice of lemon or orange.

To make a Black & Tan, pour Guinness into a chilled pilsner glass, filling it halfway. Top with Bass Ale and serve.

STEP-BY-STEP CHECKLIST

__2 DAYS BEFORE__   Reread the chapter, and make a shopping list.

__1 DAY BEFORE__   Shop (don't forget the smoked almonds, lemons, and oranges).

Prepare the cheesecake brownies; cover tightly.

Prepare the chili; refrigerate.

__MORNING OF THE PARTY__   Prepare the blue cheese dressing.

Chill the beers and glasses.

Cut up the chicken wings and refrigerate or thaw frozen precut wings.

__90 MINUTES BEFORE__   Assemble the Mega Sandwich and cover tightly; do not bake yet.

__1 HOUR BEFORE__   Prepare the Hot Wings.

__45 MINUTES BEFORE__   Bake the Hot Wings.

Slice the oranges and lemons for the beer. Slice the limes and jalapeños and chop the cilantro for the chili toppings.

30 MINUTES BEFORE — Set out the chili toppings, brownies, and blue cheese dressing on the table with plates, bowls, and napkins.

Set out the smoked almonds.

Reheat the chili.

15 MINUTES BEFORE — Bake the Mega Sandwich.

Brush the wing sauce on the Hot Wings.

Turn on the music.

AS GUESTS ARRIVE — Serve!

OPTIONAL SHORTCUTS

1. Purchase frozen chicken wings that are already cut up from a grocery or warehouse store. This is a real timesaver.

2. Purchase cookies or brownies instead of baking the cheesecake brownie bars.

3. Purchase carrot and celery sticks already cut up in a bag in the produce section.

PARTY ETIQUETTE

Whenever you are having a gathering or party that may be loud, it is considerate to tell your close neighbors in advance. Invite them to drop by the party, or tell them to feel free to let you know if the party gets too loud and you will do your best to tone down the noise.

MISTAKES TO AVOID

Never measure wet ingredients or salt directly over the mixing bowl with your ingredients. You may accidentally overpour and ruin your recipe. Pour them into the measuring cups or spoons over the sink or a small bowl and then add to your mixing bowl.

TIPS TO ENSURE SUCCESS

Having a larger gathering than the menu serves? Simply multiply the ingredients by two and double any recipe easily. Smaller crowd? Divide any recipe by two and make half.

CHAPTER 11

MY FIRST THANKSGIVING

*T*HANKSGIVING IS THE MEAL HOSTS CAN FEEL the most pressure about preparing. The entire celebration is set around the *meal*, the Thanksgiving feast! Messing it up could make for a household full of unhappy guests. Gulp! For a beginner, the pressure could be off the charts! Let me start by saying what most cooking classes and books don't tell you. Of all the meals you typically prepare in a year, this one can be the most labor-intensive. Preparing a Thanksgiving meal can be a lot of work. Every year, fantastic cooks and chefs are challenged to come up with a new take on what is a very traditional meal. They offer all types of variations and new recipes. However, since most people eat a Thanksgiving meal only once a year, they like the basics: turkey, stuffing, gravy, mashed potatoes, vegetables, rolls, and pumpkin pie for dessert. So to keep it as simple as possible, we will stick with the basics. The reason I tell you this is not to discourage you, but rather to prepare you. I like to know what I'm getting into ahead of time, so I can gird my loins for the battle!

Having said that, if you follow the step-by-step checklist, you can prepare this menu with confidence. Your meal will be delicious, and you will have much less stress because you will have paced yourself. And you will have joined the millions of home cooks nationwide who stare in disbelief when a Thanksgiving meal that has taken 3 days to prepare has been consumed in 15 minutes flat! Take it as a compliment! Your family will enjoy this meal. The little ones you have invited will have such great memories of family connection, and your guests will have one more thing to be thankful for... you!

You can serve the Thanksgiving meal "family-style," which means all the food goes on platters and in serving dishes to be passed at the table. Or you can set up the meal "buffet-style," which means you arrange all the food on the platters and serving dishes and set up an area in your kitchen or your dining room where guests take their plates and fill them at the buffet table and then return to the dinner table to eat. Buffet-style serving is a little less complicated, because you are not constantly passing dishes to others who want seconds and you don't have to reach over other people for more rolls. It is a personal preference, however.

Do have an attractive low centerpiece at the dinner and buffet table. After all, Thanksgiving is a feast. Even grocery stores have pretty arrangements in vases or cornucopias (flowers or vegetables and fruit), which are always so festive. Or use a clear glass footed bowl, such as a trifle bowl, and fill it with fruit and nuts for a simple and elegant centerpiece. If you are having a fairly large gathering, put salt and pepper, gravy, and butter at both ends of the dinner table, even if you are serving buffet style. Use a tablecloth or placemats in fall colors. If you have children attending, you could set up a card table where they can make their own placemats out of construction paper, with leaf or turkey cutouts. Coloring books and crayons are always popular. This also gives them an activity before the meal starts.

If you have a special family tradition or would like to start one, this is a perfect time. Saying grace before the meal and setting aside a time during the day when all family members in attendance can share something they are thankful for really puts the focus on the "Thanksgiving" part of the day.

MENU

Serves 8 to 10

Appetizers
Chilled Shrimp with Cocktail Sauce
Mixed nuts in the shell
Assorted cheeses and crackers

Meal
Roast Turkey with Pan Gravy
Herbed Stuffing or Apple-Pecan Stuffing
Mashed Potatoes
Butter and Brown Sugar Glazed Carrots
Crescent rolls (purchased) with butter
Pumpkin Pie with Whipped Cream

Drinks
Wine: riesling, chardonnay, pinot noir
Sparkling nonalcoholic cider
Assorted sodas, juices, and bottled water

Music Suggestions
Across the Universe Original Soundtrack (Beatles music)

Chilled Shrimp with Cocktail Sauce
Makes 8 to 10 servings

1 ½ to 2 pounds large shelled, tail-on frozen cooked shrimp (31 to 40 per pound)
1 large bottle cocktail sauce

Defrost the shrimp by placing them in a colander or strainer and running them under cold water for 8 to 10 minutes, until defrosted. Fill a large bowl with ice and place the shrimp on top. Pour the cocktail sauce into a small bowl and serve alongside the shrimp. Have a small, empty bowl available for the discarded tails.

Roast Turkey with Pan Gravy
Makes 8 to 10 servings

1 turkey, about 12 pounds, defrosted
4 tablespoons unsalted butter (½ stick), softened to room temperature
2 tablespoons dried turkey seasoning (see Note)
2 teaspoons salt
½ teaspoon freshly ground black pepper
2 cups chicken broth (soup aisle)

Gravy
4 cups water
2 medium carrots, each cut into 2 or 3 pieces
1 large onion, quartered
1 bay leaf
1 can (14 ounces) chicken broth
Reserved turkey neck and giblets
¼ cup drippings from roasted turkey
½ cup white wine

3 tablespoons all-purpose unbleached flour
½ teaspoon salt
Freshly ground black pepper to taste

Special Equipment
Instant-read thermometer

Preheat the oven to 450 degrees F. Remove the giblets (heart, kidneys, and liver) from the turkey (they are usually packed in a bag in the neck cavity). Remove the neck from the opposite cavity inside the turkey. Reserve for the gravy. Rinse the turkey inside and out in cold water and pat dry. Starting at the neck cavity, loosen the skin from the breast and drumsticks by inserting a tablespoon, upside down, under the skin, gently pushing it between the skin and meat to separate the skin. In a small bowl, combine the butter, turkey seasoning, salt, and pepper. Rub the mixture under the skin onto the breast meat and both drumsticks.

Place the turkey, breast side up, in a shallow roasting pan. Pour the broth over the turkey. Place in the oven and turn the oven temperature down to 325 degrees F. Roast for about 2 hours.

While the turkey is roasting, make the stock for the gravy. Combine the water, carrots, onion, bay leaf, chicken broth, and neck and giblets in a large saucepan and bring to a boil. Reduce the heat to low and cook until reduced to 2 ½ cups. This will take 1 to 1 ½ hours. Using a sieve, strain the stock into a medium bowl and discard the solids. Reserve until the turkey comes out of the oven.

After the turkey has roasted for 2 hours, place the instant-read thermometer in the meaty part of the thigh, making sure not to touch the bone. The turkey is done when the thermometer reads 175 to 180 degrees F. If it hasn't reached this temperature, roast it for 15 minutes more and check again. Repeat until the thermometer indicates that the turkey is done. If the skin is becoming too browned, you can tent the turkey with a piece of aluminum foil until it is finished roasting. Take the turkey out of the oven and put it on a heatproof surface. Remove ¼ cup of the turkey drippings from the bottom of the pan, cover the turkey with aluminum foil, and let it rest for 15 to 20 minutes before you carve it.

To make the gravy, while the turkey is resting, bring the wine to a boil in a medium saucepan. Combine the flour and turkey drippings in a bowl and stir with a whisk until smooth. Add to the wine and cook over medium heat for 1 minute, stirring constantly. Stir in the 2 ½ cups of strained stock, salt, and pepper to taste. Simmer over low heat for 10 to 15 minutes.

To carve the turkey, cut through the skin between the drumstick and the body. Pull the leg outward to locate the joint at the body and cut through the joint to remove the leg. This includes the thigh and the drumstick. Remove the other leg and both wings in the same way. Cut between the joint to separate the thigh and drumstick. Slice the meat off the thigh and drumstick and put it on a platter. Insert the carving fork to steady the turkey and slice the breast into thin slices, cutting parallel to the rib cage. Continue on both sides until you have enough turkey carved to serve.

Pour the gravy into a gravy boat or bowl and serve with the turkey.

Tip: To thaw a frozen turkey, make sure you purchase it by the Monday before (Thanksgiving is always on a Thursday). Thaw it in the refrigerator in its original wrap in a baking pan.

Note: The spice section of most grocery stores has prepared turkey seasoning, or you can mix together 2 teaspoons each of dried sage, dried thyme, and dried marjoram.

Herbed Stuffing
Makes 8 to 10 servings

4 tablespoons unsalted butter (½ stick)
2 cups finely chopped onion
1 cup finely chopped celery
1 cup sliced fresh mushrooms (optional)
1 package (14 ounces) cubed herb stuffing mix (such as Mrs. Cubbison's or
*   Pepperidge Farm)*
2 ½ cups chicken broth
Nonstick cooking spray

Melt the butter in a large sauté pan over medium heat. Add the onion and celery and sauté until the onions are transparent, about 5 minutes. Add the mushrooms, if desired, and sauté for 3 to 4 minutes more, stirring frequently. Pour the stuffing mix into a large bowl. Add the sautéed vegetables and stir. Add 1 ½ cups of the broth, and stir lightly. Add the remaining 1 cup broth and toss. Spray a 9-by-13-inch pan with cooking spray and spoon the stuffing into the pan. Cover and refrigerate until ready to bake.

When ready to bake, cover the pan with aluminum foil and bake at 325 degrees F for 40 to 45 minutes.

Variation: For Apple-Pecan Stuffing, omit the mushrooms and add 1 cup coarsely chopped pecans and 1 cup finely chopped apple to the stuffing.

Note: For this menu, the stuffing is baked in a pan rather than in the turkey cavity, to make the process simpler. If you prefer, stuff the turkey and adjust the roasting time, following the package directions.

Mashed Potatoes
Makes 8 to 10 servings

4 pounds Yukon Gold potatoes, peeled and cut into 1-inch cubes
1 tablespoon salt, plus more to taste
1 cup milk, plus more if necessary
½ cup half-and-half (dairy section)
4 tablespoons unsalted butter (½ stick)
Freshly ground black pepper to taste

Put the cubed potatoes and 1 tablespoon salt in a large pan and add water to cover the potatoes by 1 inch. Bring to a boil over medium-high heat, reduce the heat to low, and simmer until the potatoes are tender when stuck with a fork, 18 to 20 minutes. Do not overcook. Drain well in a colander.

Transfer to a large bowl. In a separate small bowl, microwave the 1 cup milk, half-and-half, and butter on medium-high power for 1 to 2 minutes, or until hot. Carefully pour over the potatoes and either mash with a hand masher or use a hand mixer to mash the potatoes. If you need a little more milk, add a few tablespoons at a time until the potatoes are the desired consistency. Mash until the lumps are gone, but do not overmix or the potatoes will become starchy. Add salt and pepper to taste, and serve immediately.

Butter and Brown Sugar Glazed Carrots
Makes 8 to 10 servings

6 cups peeled, thinly sliced carrots
½ teaspoon salt, plus more to taste
3 tablespoons unsalted butter
⅔ cup brown sugar
Freshly ground black pepper to taste

Place the carrots in 1 inch of water in a large saucepan with ½ teaspoon salt. Bring to a boil, turn the heat down to low, cover, and simmer for 13 to 15 minutes. Check halfway through to make sure the water has not boiled away, adding a little more if necessary. Drain the carrots in a colander. In the same saucepan, heat the butter and brown sugar over medium heat for 1 minute, stirring constantly. Add the carrots and cook for 3 to 5 minutes, until the carrots are glazed. Season with salt and pepper to taste.

Pumpkin Pie with Whipped Cream
Makes 8 servings

1 can (16 ounces) pumpkin
¾ cup sugar
1 teaspoon ground cinnamon
½ teaspoon ground ginger
⅛ teaspoon ground cloves
¼ teaspoon ground nutmeg, plus more for sprinkling
3 eggs
1 ⅔ cups evaporated milk (see Note)
1 purchased 9-inch pie crust (refrigerated or frozen food section)
1 can whipped cream or 2 cups nondairy whipped topping

Preheat the oven to 375 degrees F. In a large mixing bowl, combine the pumpkin, sugar, cinnamon, ginger, cloves, and nutmeg. Whisk in the eggs and slowly stir in the evaporated milk. Mix well. Place the pie crust in a 9-inch pie pan, if it is not sold in a pan, and pour in the pumpkin filling. Make 3 strips of aluminum foil, each about 1 to 2 inches wide. Crimp the foil strips around the edges of the pie crust to prevent burning. Bake for 30 minutes. Remove the foil strips and bake for 20 minutes more. Test for doneness by inserting a butter knife into the center of the pie. If the pie is done, it will come out clean. If it does not, bake for 5 to 7 minutes more and check again for doneness. Cool completely and serve with whipped cream sprinkled with a bit of the ground nutmeg. If you won't be serving the pie within 2 hours of baking, cover and refrigerate. Refrigerate any leftovers. (What leftovers?) For two pies, double the recipe.

Note: Evaporated milk is sold in cans, usually on the coffee aisle of grocery stores. Do not use sweetened condensed milk.

STEP-BY-STEP CHECKLIST

___3 DAYS BEFORE___   Reread the recipes and make a shopping list.

Shop. Don't forget drinks, 3 tubes crescent rolls (from the refrigerated section), mixed nuts (from the produce section), butter, cheese, and crackers.

Defrost the turkey in a pan in the refrigerator.

___2 DAYS BEFORE___   Clean the house.

Prepare a craft for kids (optional).

___1 DAY BEFORE___   Prepare the pumpkin pie, cover, and refrigerate.

Chop the ingredients for the stuffing, cover, and refrigerate.

Set the table.

Pick up an autumn arrangement for the table.

Chill the drinks.

___THANKSGIVING MORNING___   Prepare the turkey. For a 2:00 dinner time, begin roasting at about 11:30 a.m. in a preheated oven.

Prepare the stock for the gravy, strain, discard the giblets, and set aside.

Prepare the stuffing, cover, and refrigerate.

145

Set out the mixed nuts with a couple of nutcrackers in a bowl. Have an empty bowl nearby for discarded shells.

1 HOUR BEFORE

Peel, wash, cube, and cook the potatoes.

Bake the stuffing.

Slice the carrots, and put them on the stove with the water. Do not cook yet.

Defrost and serve the shrimp and cocktail sauce. Set out cheese and crackers.

30 MINUTES BEFORE

Check the turkey with the thermometer; take it out of the oven when done, and cover with aluminum foil.

Prepare the gravy, cover, and set aside.

Put the crescent rolls on baking sheets.

15 MINUTES BEFORE

Cook the carrots, glaze, cover, and set aside.

Mash the potatoes, cover, and set aside.

Take the stuffing out of the oven.

Bake the crescent rolls, following the package directions.

Carve the turkey.

Serve!

OPTIONAL SHORTCUTS

1. Purchase your pie(s) instead of baking if time is tight.

2. Purchase a bag of peeled, sliced carrots that yields 6 cups and presliced mushrooms (if using for the stuffing) instead of peeling and slicing your own.

3. Purchase fresh-baked dinner rolls instead of baking crescent rolls.

PARTY ETIQUETTE

Most guests will ask if you'd like them to bring something to the meal. It is perfectly acceptable to allow your guests to bring a favorite dish, appetizer, drinks, or dessert. This can take some of the pressure off so you can concentrate on the main meal items. If they offer to help clean up after the feast, graciously accept!

MISTAKES TO AVOID

Don't get too stressed! Pulling off a Thanksgiving meal is like conducting a symphony. Just as a conductor skillfully brings in each instrument at the proper time to achieve a spectacular musical experience, you prepare each recipe according to the checklist to achieve all the dishes that contribute to a delicious feast for your loved ones. This takes calm, organized preparation. Bravo to you for your efforts!

TIPS TO ENSURE SUCCESS

If you have someone available to help you prepare for this meal, enlist their services. They can chop ingredients for recipes and keep the dishes clean so the kitchen stays organized while you are cooking.

CHAPTER 12

CHRISTMAS SEASON SOCIAL

*T*HE CHRISTMAS SEASON IS A WONDERFUL TIME to have family, neighbors, co-workers, and friends into your home for good cheer. It is also an opportunity to extend your hospitality to those who aren't in your usual circle of friends, but who might be alone at Christmas. Think of the new couple down the street who relocated from another area. How about the disabled neighbor or the elderly widow living alone? The Christmas season can be a lonely time for many people, and inviting someone you know of to your home for a friendly evening can truly lift their spirits.

When I was younger, I always tried to have the perfect "Currier & Ives" type of Christmas. In other words, I wanted to have the house decorated stem to stern, the 10 varieties of Christmas cookies baked, the perfect presents for everyone, and so on. I really drove myself crazy and was usually in for a let-down.

Now I focus on a few things for the Christmas season that I try to do really well. For instance, one year I will concentrate on serving loved ones with a special dinner at my home, but I will bake few or no cookies that year and pare down on the Christmas gifts. The next year I may want to concentrate on baking cookies, so I bake a lot and give them as gifts, but I won't be hosting any big get-togethers. Another year I may concentrate my time on a project that involves serving the needy, so I will host a simple family gathering and keep any decorating to a minimum. In other words, some years ago, it finally dawned on me that happy Christmas memories are an accumulation of many years of a few special things each year. It is not trying to achieve the unrealistic, storybook Christmas every single year, which burns out and exhausts scores of well-meaning people like me.

So if this is your year to spend some of your efforts on having a gathering in your home, be realistic and simplify in other areas so you can enjoy yourself. You don't want Christmas to be a blur of exhausting activity that leaves you needing a week to recuperate when it is over. Prioritize and concentrate your efforts on the most important areas.

This menu is perfect to serve buffet style. Serve the baked Brie as an appetizer with a cup of eggnog or Pomegranate Sparkling Punch. The homemade buttermilk biscuits are a treat served as small sandwiches filled with slices of ham or turkey breast. Add honey mustard, orange marmalade, or cranberry chutney for a satisfying little entrée. The Cheddar Hash Brown Gratin is creamy and cheesy. The Pear, Blue Cheese, and Candied Almond Salad is a nice winter salad because pears are in season and taste great with the bite of blue cheese and sweetness of candied almonds. Finally, enjoy the delicate scent of the Orange Rum Sauce drizzled on a slice of rich Eggnog Cake for dessert.

MENU

Serves 10 to 12

Baked Brie in Crescent Dough

Buttermilk Biscuits with Ham and/or Turkey

Cheddar Hash Brown Gratin

Pear, Blue Cheese, and Candied Almond Salad with Champagne Vinaigrette

Eggnog Cake with Orange Rum Sauce

Drinks

Eggnog

Pomegranate Sparkling Punch

Wines: zinfandel, chardonnay

Music

Noel by Josh Grobin

A Charlie Brown Christmas by Vince Guaraldi (jazz)

Baked Brie in Crescent Dough
Makes 10 to 12 servings

Nonstick cooking spray
1 tube crescent roll dough (refrigerated section)
1 wheel Brie cheese (19.6 ounces)
1 egg
1 teaspoon water

Preheat the oven to 350 degrees F. Spray a baking sheet with cooking spray. Open the crescent dough and smooth it out. Pinch together all of the perforated seams with your fingers to make 1 piece of dough. It will be a rectangular shape. With a sharp knife, cut off about 1 inch of the dough to make it a square. Reserve this scrap of dough. Unwrap the Brie and place it in the middle of the dough. Stretching the dough slightly to fit, wrap it up around the Brie and pinch the seams together to completely wrap the Brie in the dough. Pinch together at the top. I cut out small shapes (such as leaves or bells) from the reserved scrap of dough and press them onto the dough to cover the top seam. Beat the egg with the water in a small bowl and, using a pastry or barbecue basting brush, lightly brush the beaten egg on the dough. This will give it a nice shine when it is baked. Bake for 12 to 18 minutes and serve immediately on a pretty platter. Cut a small wedge and let the melted cheese ooze out a bit. Serve with a cheese knife and spoon on the platter so guests can serve themselves.

Buttermilk Biscuits with Ham and/or Turkey
Makes 36 biscuits

Biscuits
8 cups all-purpose unbleached flour
4 teaspoons baking powder
½ teaspoon baking soda
2 teaspoons salt
1 tablespoon sugar
1 cup cold unsalted butter (2 sticks), cut into small pieces
4 cups buttermilk

Sandwiches
3- to 4-pound honey ham or Black Forest ham, sliced
3- to 4-pound boneless cooked turkey breast, sliced
Honey mustard
Orange marmalade
Cranberry chutney
Fresh parsley, for garnish

To make the biscuits, preheat the oven to 450 degrees F. In a large bowl, sift together the flour, baking powder, baking soda, salt, and sugar. To sift, hold a strainer over your mixing bowl. Measure the dry ingredients into the strainer and tap it with a butter knife to sift the mixture into the bowl. This will yield lighter biscuits. With a pastry blender, cut the small pieces of butter into the flour mixture until it resembles small peas. If you do not have a pastry cutter, take a butter knife in each hand and, with a crisscross motion, cut the butter into the flour over and over until it is cut into pea-size pieces and blended with the flour. This will take a minute or two.

Add the buttermilk and, with a spoon, mix together until a dough forms. Sprinkle a bit of flour on a cutting board or flat surface and knead the dough with the heel of your hand 5 or 6 times, no more. Using a rolling pin, roll the dough out ¾ inch thick. With a 2 ½-inch round biscuit cutter or 2 ½-inch diameter drinking glass dipped in flour, cut out biscuits and place them on an ungreased baking sheet. Immediately bake for 10 to 12 minutes, or until golden brown.

To make the sandwiches, cut the biscuits in half and fill each with 2 or 3 slices of ham or turkey. Arrange on a platter, garnished with fresh parsley. Transfer the honey mustard, orange marmalade, and cranberry chutney from jars to pretty bowls with knives or spoons so guests can add some to their biscuits.

Cheddar Hash Brown Gratin
Makes 10 to 12 servings

Nonstick cooking spray
4 cups shredded sharp Cheddar cheese
½ cup finely chopped white onion
2 teaspoons salt
¼ teaspoon freshly ground black pepper
¼ cup fresh flat-leaf (Italian) parsley, chopped
4 tablespoons unsalted butter (½ stick)
¼ cup all-purpose unbleached flour
1 ½ cups milk, warmed in the microwave for 45 seconds
2 bags (32 ounces each) frozen hash browns

Preheat the oven to 350 degrees. Spray a 4-quart oven-safe casserole dish with cooking spray. Mix the cheese, onion, salt, pepper, and parsley in a medium mixing bowl. Melt the butter in the microwave for 15 seconds in a separate medium bowl. Add the flour and mix well. Whisk the milk into the butter and flour.

Put one third of the hash browns in the casserole dish. Top with one third of the cheese mixture. Repeat 2 more times with the remaining hash browns and cheese mixture. Pour the flour, butter, and milk mixture on top. Cover with a lid or aluminum foil and bake for 40 minutes. Uncover and bake for 20 minutes longer, until brown.

Pear, Blue Cheese, and Candied Almond Salad with Champagne Vinaigrette
Makes 10 to 12 servings

Champagne Vinaigrette

½ cup extra virgin olive oil
2 tablespoons champagne vinegar or apple cider vinegar (condiments aisle)
1 ½ teaspoons Dijon mustard
½ teaspoon sugar
¼ teaspoon salt
Freshly ground black pepper

Salad

3 heads romaine lettuce, washed and chopped, or 2 bags (10 ounces each)
*   prepared chopped romaine*
1 red pear, thinly sliced
1 green pear, thinly sliced
¾ cup crumbled blue cheese
¾ cup candied sliced almonds (produce section)

To make the vinaigrette, whisk together the oil, vinegar, mustard, sugar, salt, and pepper.

To make the salad, in a large salad bowl, combine the romaine, sliced pears, blue cheese, and candied almonds. Toss with the vinaigrette. Serve immediately.

Tip: When purchasing pears, look for ones that are fragrant and give slightly when squeezed lightly. If they are still hard, purchase them a few days before, put them in a brown lunch bag, and store in a dark cupboard to ripen.

155

Eggnog Cake with Orange Rum Sauce

Makes 10 to 12 servings

Nonstick cooking spray
½ cup finely chopped pecans
1 box yellow cake mix
1 cup purchased eggnog
¼ cup canola oil
¼ cup water
3 large eggs
1 tablespoon dark rum
¼ teaspoon ground nutmeg

Orange Rum Sauce

4 tablespoons unsalted butter (½ stick)
1 cup orange juice
½ cup powdered sugar
¼ cup rum
1 tablespoon cornstarch
2 tablespoons cold water

Special Equipment

10-inch Bundt pan

Preheat the oven to 350 degrees. Spray the Bundt pan generously with cooking spray and sprinkle the chopped pecans in the bottom of the pan. Set aside. In a large bowl, mix the cake mix, eggnog, oil, water, eggs, rum, and nutmeg and beat with an electric mixer on medium speed for 2 minutes. Pour the batter into the pan and bake for 55 to 60 minutes, or until a toothpick inserted in the cake comes out clean (there should be no runny batter).

Cool for 10 minutes. With oven mitts, put a plate on top of the Bundt pan and quickly turn it over, releasing the cake from the pan to the plate. Cool the cake.

To make the sauce, melt the butter in a saucepan. Stir in the orange juice and sugar until dissolved. Add the rum. Mix the cornstarch in the cold water in a separate mixing cup until dissolved. Add to the sauce. Stir until thickened, about 1 minute. Remove from the heat. Cover and chill. Serve over cake slices.

Pomegranate Sparkling Punch
Makes about 4 quarts

2 quarts pomegranate juice
1 quart orange juice
1 liter lemon-lime soda

Mix the juices and soda together and serve in a punch bowl.

STEP-BY-STEP CHECKLIST

2 DAYS BEFORE Clean the house, reread the recipes, and make a shopping list.

1 DAY BEFORE Shop; don't forget wine and eggnog.

Prepare the Champagne Vinaigrette; refrigerate.

Set up the buffet table.

Chill the drinks.

MORNING OF THE PARTY Prepare the Eggnog Cake; cover.

Make the Cheddar Hash Brown Gratin; refrigerate (do not bake).

Chop the romaine, if necessary; cover and refrigerate.

Prepare the biscuits, bake, cool, and cover tightly.

Prepare the Orange Rum Sauce; refrigerate.

1 HOUR BEFORE Assemble the biscuit and ham/turkey sandwiches and garnish with the fresh parsley; place on a platter and cover.

Set out the honey mustard, cranberry chutney, and orange marmalade.

Set out the Eggnog Cake.

Preheat the oven and bake the Cheddar Hash Brown Gratin.

30 MINUTES BEFORE Prepare the Baked Brie in Crescent Dough.

Take the Champagne Vinaigrette out of the refrigerator.

15 MINUTES BEFORE Bake the Brie.

Slice the pears and assemble the salad; do not add the vinaigrette yet.

Prepare the punch.

Turn on the music.

AS GUESTS ARRIVE Serve the Brie, punch, and eggnog.

Toss the salad.

Take the Cheddar Hash Brown Gratin out of the oven.

Serve.

OPTIONAL SHORTCUTS

1. If you would like more desserts, ask your guests to each bring 1 dozen of their favorite Christmas cookies.

2. Purchase biscuits from your bakery or frozen food section of the grocery store instead of making them. Purchase them the day of or no earlier than one day before your social.

PARTY ETIQUETTE

When you have been to someone's home for a nice dinner, it is always polite to call or write a thank-you note afterwards expressing appreciation for your host's kindness and hospitality. Reciprocating by extending *your* hospitality to them is likewise a kind and welcomed thing to do.

MISTAKES TO AVOID

Make sure your measurements are accurate. Whenever you use a dry measuring cup, use a butter knife to level it off for accuracy. When using a liquid measuring cup, put it on a flat surface and bend down to look at the side of it for accurate measuring. Sloppy measuring will give you inconsistent results in your recipes

TIPS TO ENSURE SUCCESS

The secret to delicious homemade biscuits is to use well-chilled butter. Work quickly and don't overmix the dough so the butter stays cold. Try to get the biscuits into the preheated oven as soon as possible after placing them on the baking sheets.

CLOSING THOUGHTS

*I*F THERE IS ONE COMMON THREAD IN THIS BOOK, it is the idea that hospitality is an art practiced for the benefit of guests. Today it is not uncommon for events like wedding receptions and birthday parties to be completely planned and centered on the bride and groom and the birthday celebrant. I believe this misses the mark entirely. I realize this may seem like a shocking statement, but bear with me. Think instead of this motivation:

The parents of the bride (or the couple themselves) are so thankful for a deep, committed love that results in a marriage union that their appreciation and joy are evident. They desire to celebrate the blessed event of the marriage ceremony by asking their family and friends to witness the exchanging of the vows. In addition, they invite family and friends to share in the joy and bless the couple with their presence at a party or reception in the couple's honor. The ensuing party should be planned with the *guests* in mind, not necessarily the couple.

The *guests* are the ones who are focused on the *couple*. They attend a bridal shower to provide the couple with gifts to help set up their household; they purchase a wedding gift (often from a gift registry of specific items that the couple desire); they set aside their time to witness the vows and help celebrate the marriage union. But *they* are the ones who are focused on the couple, not the couple themselves or their parents. The parents or the couple—that is, the hosts—are focused on the *guests!* The hosts' desire is that the guests will feel honored and valued by the couple for supporting them and sharing their special day, so the party or reception is planned to meet this motivation.

The same motivation is ideal for a birthday party. The host is focused on the *guests,* who attend because they are sharing their lives to help celebrate a very important day: the day of a loved one's birth! The guests will be focused on the birthday celebrant by purchasing a gift and attending the party.

I take the time to reiterate the importance of motivation when you entertain because it is the foundation of the entire event. Anything else you build will rest upon your motivation.

With that in mind, my hope is that this book will be genuinely useful to you. When you ask just about anyone to list their top priorities, most would have family and friends near the top. What better way to put that love for family and friends into action than to extend a cordial and generous reception and treatment to them? I believe anyone can learn to extend this hospitality with a bit of direction, patience, and practice. You have a lot to offer, and I am confident that you are able! Developing your gifts and talents and expressing your creativity in a way that adds to the richness and happiness of those you care about is an endeavor worthy of your time. It is a wealthy family indeed whose members value extending hospitality to one another.

I wish you many happy and fruitful hours entertaining in your home with your loved ones.

Cordially,

Patricia Mendez

KITCHEN BASICS

USEFUL KITCHEN ITEMS TO HAVE ON HAND for the recipes in this book:

- Electric hand mixer
- Blender
- Hand grater
- Hand juicer
- Melon baller
- Nutcracker
- Vegetable peeler
- Liquid measuring cup
- Dry measuring cups
- Measuring spoons
- Whisk
- Good-quality chef's knife
- 8-by-8-inch square baking pan
- Two 9-inch round baking pans
- 9-by-13-inch baking pan

- 9-inch quiche, tart, or pie pan
- Muffin pan
- 10-inch Bundt or tube cake pan
- 2 or 3 baking or cookie sheets
- Large roasting pan for turkey
- 1 set small, medium, and large mixing bowls
- Apron
- Kitchen timer
- Rolling pin
- Pastry cutter
- Pastry brush
- Cutting board
- Strainer
- Martini shaker

Basic Chicken

3 chicken breasts
6 chicken thighs
Olive oil
Salt and freshly ground pepper to taste

Preheat the oven to 375 degrees F. Place the chicken on a baking sheet and rub with olive oil. Salt and pepper generously. Bake for 35 to 40 minutes, or until baked through. Cool, remove the skin, and shred all the chicken meat. Discard the skin and bones.

Note: This recipe can be used—if you cannot find a purchased rotisserie chicken from a grocery store—for the following recipes:

- Chicken Tortilla Soup
- Chicken Salad with Grapes and Walnuts on Mini-Croissants

CONVERSION CHARTS

OVEN TEMPERATURES

FAHRENHEIT	CELSIUS
250	120
275	140
300	150
325	160
350	180
375	190
400	200
425	220
450	230
475	240
500	260

EQUIVALENTS (APPROXIMATE)

1 egg white	2 tablespoons
1 egg yolk	1 tablespoons
1 large egg	3 tablespoons
1 cup grated cheese	4 ounces
1 cup sugar	8 ounces
1 cup powdered sugar	4 ½ ounces
1 cup flour (sifted)	5 ounces
1 stick butter	8 tablespoons or 4 ounces or ½ cup

LIQUID CONVERSIONS

U.S.	IMPERIAL	METRIC
2 tablespoons	1 fluid ounce	30 milliliters
3 tablespoons	1 ½ fluid ounces	45 milliliters
¼ cup	2 fluid ounces	60 milliliters
⅓ cup	2 ½ fluid ounces	75 milliliters
½ cup	4 fluid ounces	125 milliliters
⅔ cup	5 fluid ounces	150 milliliters
¾ cup	6 fluid ounces	175 milliliters
1 cup	8 fluid ounces	250 milliliters
1 ¼ cups	10 fluid ounces	300 milliliters
1 ⅓ cups	11 fluid ounces	325 milliliters
1 ½ cups	12 fluid ounces	350 milliliters
1 ⅔ cups	13 fluid ounces	375 milliliters
1 ¾ cups	14 fluid ounces	400 milliliters
2 cups (1 pint)	16 fluid ounces	500 milliliters
2 ½ cups	20 fluid ounces (1 pint)	600 milliliters
3 ¾ cups	1 ½ pints	900 milliliters
4 cups	1 ¾ pints	1 liter

ACKNOWLEDGMENTS

SPECIAL THANKS TO:

Cindy Bero for your thoughtful input, suggested revisions, and faithful friendship.

Judith Legg for your first round of thorough editing.

Martin Mendez for your wise suggestions, practical help with the interior photographs (by no means a small task), and unwavering support throughout the entire project.

Rene Gonzalez for your assistance and use of your photography equipment for the interior photographs.

Virginia and Leotis Hobbs for your kindness and outstanding proficiency with the cover and author photographs.

John Peirce for your valuable friendship, generosity, and skill with the photography.

Lionel Henderson for your expertise with graphic design for the logo.

Dotti Albertine, Rebecca Pepper, and Laren Bright. You are all accomplished professionals whose gifts and talents added significant quality to this book.

All the fantastic home cooks in my family. Thank you for your example of hospitality and for all the delicious meals over the years!

INDEX